all dogs need some training

all dogs need some training

Liz Palika

Illustrations by Pam Posey-Tanzey

Howell Book House
New York

Howell Book House
A Simon & Schuster Macmillan Company
1633 Broadway
New York, NY 10019

MACMILLAN is a registered trademark of Macmillan, Inc.

Library of Congress Cataloging-in-Publication Data:

Palika, Liz, 1954-
  All dogs need some training / Liz Palika.
      p.   cm.
  ISBN: 0-87605-407-6
  1. Dogs--Training.   I. Title.
SF431.P33   1997
636.7' 0835--dc21   97-6183
                                                                CIP

        00 01 02 03 04 05 QWF 10 9 8 7 6

Interpretation of the printing code: the rightmost number of the first series of numbers is the year of the book's printing; the rightmost number of the second series of numbers is the number of the book's printing. For example, a printing code of 97-1 shows that the first printing occurred in 1997.

Printed in the United States of America

Design by Amy Peppler Adams—designLab, Seattle

Dedication

This book is dedicated to Ursa, an Australian Shepherd, who has been my dog training class demonstration dog for over nine years. Ursa is a therapy dog, pulls a wagon, competes in obedience, loves flyball and agility, lets kids climb all over her, and corrects wayward puppies with calm and grace. Ursa was a challenging puppy herself, and at times I was ready to pull my hair out over some of her escapades. However, she grew up to be a wonderful friend and companion, and over the years she has taught me much.

Thanks, Ursa.

Table of Contents

Introduction

Dogs have been a big part of my life for as long as I can remember, and according to some family photos, even before that. Because of my professions (dog trainer and writer), my dogs are with me almost twenty-four hours a day and we do a lot of things together. A dog (or two) goes for a walk with me every morning and trots alongside my bicycle each afternoon. When I buy mulch, potting soil or a forty-pound bag of dog food, a dog pulls the wagon from my van to the backyard or house. My dogs and I do therapy dog work, agility, play Frisbee and tennis ball games and much, much more. My dogs can do all these things with me because they are trained; they know the rules, accept them and follow them.

I have been teaching dog owners how to train their dogs for over twenty years. I want the dog owner to understand what his or her dog is, why the dog acts the way it does and that chewing up the couch was not a personal attack. When the owner understands his dog and learns how to teach the dog simply, humanely and effectively, both parties will succeed.

In my classes, I have had a few simple goals. I want to teach the basic obedience commands, of course, but I would also like to save some dogs from a life of boredom locked in the backyard. I would like to save the lives of some dogs who might otherwise be euthanized simply for a lack of time and training. I would like to prevent injuries to people because of ignorance on their part or from a lack of socialization and/or training on the dog's part.

In short, I wish every dog owner could enjoy the same relationship with their dogs that I have with mine!

Sincerely,
Liz and my constant companions, Ursa and Dax

CHAPTER 1

All Dogs (and Their Owners) Need Some Training

Why did you get a dog? If you're like most people, you wanted a dog to be a companion, a friend, a confidante and a protector. You probably wanted someone to play with and perhaps even a jogging partner. That's asking a lot of anyone; even our human best friends couldn't be all of these things. However, if you help him, a dog can be all those things to you.

Does Your Dog Need Training?

Many dog owners don't think their dogs need training. "He does just about everything I ask," they say, or "If it isn't broken, don't fix it!" Yet when owners are asked specific questions, different answers surface. "Oh well, yes, I do have to put him outside when we eat because he does beg. And sometimes he jumps on Grandma—but he doesn't jump on me!"

All dogs (and their owners) can benefit from dog training. The basic obedience commands have practical applications for all dogs. A dog in training learns to sit (on the owner's first command, not the tenth or thirteenth) and learns to sit for petting, for treats, for meals and before coming in the door. Other basic commands include lay down, stay, come and heel.

Dogs in training also learn the rules of acceptable behavior, at home and out in public. The owners learn how to teach their dog, how to praise him and how to motivate him to be good. They also learn how to prevent mistakes from happening and how to correct the mistakes that do occur.

Do you still have doubts that your dog could benefit from training?

- Does your dog jump on people?

- Does your dog pull on the leash?

- Does your dog dash through any open door?

- Does he come when you call him? (Every time you call him, not just once in a while?)

- When you call him, does he play keep-away, staying just out of reach?

- Does he steal food from the baby or off the coffee table?

- Does he dig up the backyard?

- Do your neighbors complain about his barking?

- Does he chew on inappropriate things—such as the furniture, your shoes, the kids' toys and your potted plants?

- Does he mouth your hands or grab at your clothes?

- Does he bark at and jump on your guests?

- Does he bark at other dogs?

- Does he ignore you? Or even worse, does he growl at you?

The dog who destroys your house every time you leave isn't much fun to have around. The veterinary bills that can result from your dog raiding the trash can, chewing up your sofa or eating something found in the garage aren't fun either. However, a knowledgeable owner and a trained dog can prevent these things from happening.

The Benefits of Training

The dog who drags you down the street when you try to go for a relaxing walk is going to be left alone in the backyard because it won't take long for you to get tired of the sore arms and shoulders, not to mention the embarrassment! A trained dog can go places. He can go for a walk in public; he can go hiking or camping; or go with the family on a picnic.

A trained dog will be welcome in more places and will meet new friends. When the trained dog meets those new friends, he will sit quietly while they pet him instead of jumping up on them. A trained dog has opportunities not open to the untrained dog; he can participate in dog activities and sports, such as agility, flyball, carting, Frisbee, therapy dog visits and much more.

A trained dog is also safe. The trained dog will not dash out the front door into the path of a car. The trained dog will come when he's called instead of chasing the neighbor's cat. The trained dog will lay down and stay when you tell him to instead of cutting his pads on the shattered glass from the dish you accidentally dropped on the kitchen floor.

Dog training is much more than the traditional sit, lay down, stay and come, all performed on leash every day for fifteen minutes. Dog training means teaching your dog that he's living in your house, not you in his. It means that you can set some rules for your dog and he's expected to follow those rules. Training will not turn your dog into a furry little robot, but it will cause your dog to look at you in a new light.

Training will cause you to think about him differently, too. Dog training is not something that you do to your dog; instead, it is something you and your dog do together. When you train, you learn how to teach your dog and how to motivate him so that he wants to be good. You also learn how to stop unwanted behavior, how to prevent it from happening and how to correct your dog effectively and humanely. During the training process, you also learn how much to expect from him.

Dog ownership brings with it a host of benefits. Owning a dog can provide the owner with a positive self-image, especially if the owner can display a well-behaved, attractive, healthy dog. A protective dog can increase the owner's sense of safety. The dog's sense of play and need for exercise can stimulate an owner into getting out of the recliner and away from the television. Dogs are great emotional buffers, too, and are nonjudgmental and never criticize. Training a dog requires patience, persistence and perseverance—all useful, necessary skills!

Researchers have also found that dogs are good for people. Pet owners are more likely to survive a heart attack than people who do not own pets. Pet owners have a more positive outlook on life and have more friends. Researchers also say that pet owners have lower blood pressure than people who do not own pets. However, I'll bet that if all the facts were known, the blood pressure of those people who own untrained dogs is sky-high! Coming home from a hard day's work to find the sofa destroyed and the trash spread all over the living room would be enough to give anyone high blood pressure.

Training helps establish a good relationship with your dog; a relationship built on trust, affection and respect. Training can help your dog become your best friend—a well-mannered companion who is a joy to spend time with—and one who won't raise your blood pressure.

CHAPTER 2

Teach Your Dog Simply, Humanely and Effectively

©PAM POSEY-TANZEY

As you start training Champ, you will need to remember that he wasn't born understanding English, Spanish, French, German or any other human language. He wasn't born understanding human body language, either. He was born knowing canine communication. When he bit his mom's ear and she growled, he knew instinctively that was a correction. When one of his littermates barked in a high-pitched tone of voice and wagged her tail, Champ knew that was an invitation to play.

Now that he is living with you, Champ must take everything you do and say and translate it. And his translations are based on his understanding of canine body language and verbalizations. For example, one day you might walk into the bedroom and see that Champ has chewed on one of your new leather shoes. You are angry because they were brand-new, expensive shoes and you really liked them, so you start yelling. As you are yelling, your voice gets shriller and higher pitched. You pick up the shoe and shake it in Champ's face as you continue to yell. At this point, Champ is probably getting a little confused because to him, a high-pitched voice is, depending on the tone and the situation, either the reaction to hurt or a play invitation. But your body language doesn't fit either of those reactions. Plus, when something is shaken in front of Champ's face, it's usually an invitation to play. But when he reaches out to grab the shoe, you just yell more. So Champ continues to watch you, and as he does, he gets more and more confused.

You can see by this example how frustrated, confused and mixed up our dogs can become. As you start to train Champ, your goal is to make communication as simple as possible. It's not Champ's job to make you understand, although he does that pretty well. After all, he brings you the ball when he wants to play, his bowl when he's hungry and his leash when he wants to go for a walk. So how do you communicate and teach him?

Teach a Vocabulary

As you begin to teach Champ, have a family meeting and decide on a vocabulary for Champ. What words do you want Champ to understand? Some words will be very basic, like "sit" and "lay down." But what words do you want to use to teach Champ not to jump on you or to get off the furniture? If you say "down" for lay down, you cannot then use it for getting off the furniture or for not jumping. Champ doesn't understand that many words have more than one meaning. Instead, you might want to use "lay down," "off the furniture" and "no jump."

Once you have a variety of words that you feel will cover most of Champ's actions around the house, out in the yard, in the car and out in public, then make a list of those words. Give each family member a copy of the list or post it on the refrigerator so that everyone in the family will teach Champ the same vocabulary.

When teaching Champ what these words mean, use the words as you help Champ to do what you are asking him to do. For example, to teach him that "off the furniture" means get off the sofa, tell him, "Champ, off the furniture!" as you take him by the collar and help him down. When he's on the floor, walk him away and praise him. Better yet, take him over to his blanket and tell him to lay down there and then praise him again.

During the learning process, don't keep repeating the words over and over. The words (or sounds) have no meaning for Champ until he learns what they are. So instead of sounding like the proverbial broken record, tell Champ once, then help him do whatever it is you are telling him to do. When he does it, even with your help, praise him.

Even after Champ has learned the command, you shouldn't repeat it over and over. If Champ ignores you or pretends he doesn't hear you, tell him once, then help him do it. If you allow him to ignore you while you continue to repeat the command, waiting for Champ to acknowledge you, you are teaching him that he can ignore you, that you won't follow through with a command and that he can do what he wants. Not a good lesson for Champ to learn!

When Champ Does Something Right

Most of us work better for praise than we do for criticism, and Champ is no different. When Champ does something right and you tell him, "Good boy! Yeah!" and pop a treat in his mouth, he will be much more likely to do the same thing again.

Positive reinforcement such as praise, petting and treats gives Champ the motivation to do the things you ask him to do. Champ doesn't know why you ask him to sit, nor does he understand why it seems to be so important to you. However, if you reward him every time he sits, then the sit will start to be more important to him, too!

The positive reinforcement you use should be something that Champ likes. Offering him a treat he doesn't care about will not work. Instead, use a special treat he really enjoys and then save that for your training sessions. If Champ is excited by tennis balls or toys, use those as rewards. If Champ's favorite thing in the whole world is to be scratched behind his left ear, do that! But most importantly, always use your voice when you praise Champ, "Good boy! Yeah! Super job!"

©PAM POSEY-TANZEY

Give Permission

When you see Champ about to do something that you approve of, give him permission to do it, "Champ, lay down. Good boy to lay down!" or "Bring me the ball. Good boy to bring me the ball!" Sure, Champ was going to do it anyway, but by giving him permission, you gave him a chance to do something for you. In addition, it gave you a chance to praise him.

When Champ Makes a Mistake

A correction is something you will use to let Champ know that he has made a mistake. For most dogs, your voice is the best correction. Use a deeper tone of voice to tell Champ what he has done wrong, "No jump!" or "No! Off the furniture!"

If Champ has learned to ignore your verbal corrections, then use his leash to teach him to listen to you. A leash correction is a snap and release of the leash. The snap-and-release motion is like that of a bouncing ball—an up and down movement of the hand. Snap (up) and release (down). Do not pull the leash tight and hold it there. No one learns by choking, and if the leash and collar are tight on Champ's neck, he will start to choke.

The collar you use on Champ could be one of several different types of training tools available. Most puppies start with a regular buckle collar. This is a soft collar, doesn't give a hard correction and can be bought at any pet store. However, as Champ gets bigger and stronger, he may simply push into the buckle collar and ignore any correction you try to administer. You can then switch him over to a training collar, commonly called a choke chain. Because this collar works in a slip motion and can potentially choke Champ, it should be left on him *only* when Champ is under your direct supervision. *Always* take it off him when you cannot watch him. Other training tools are available (head halters and prong collars, to name two) but should be used only with an obedience instructor's supervision, because some special skills are needed to use them properly.

To use a leash correction, the leash must be attached to Champ's collar. If Champ is in the house with you and you can supervise him to make sure it doesn't get tangled, attach the leash to his buckle collar and let him drag it around. When he makes a mistake, such as getting into the trash can or climbing up on the sofa, give him a verbal correction. Then if he ignores you, grab the leash and, using a snap-and-release motion, correct him again.

Sometimes it won't be possible for Champ to wear his leash. Perhaps you can't watch him closely enough to make sure he doesn't get it tangled. But just because Champ isn't wearing his leash doesn't mean you can't correct him if he makes a mistake.

Fill a squirt bottle with water, adding just a touch of vinegar. When Champ decides to ignore you, squirt toward him so that he can smell the vinegar water. For example, let's say Champ is off leash in the house when your neighbor comes over and knocks on the door. Champ dashes to the door, barking. Now if you start yelling at him to be quiet, he's just going to bark more. After all, to him, your yelling is just like his barking! However, if you tell him in a normal tone of voice, "Champ, quiet!" and squirt him with the vinegar water, he's going to stop barking as he tries to lick the vinegar water off his nose. At that point you can tell him, "Good boy to be quiet!"

When you are trying to correct Champ, never hit him, either with your hand, a rolled-up newspaper or magazine, flyswatter or anything else. Don't throw things at him. Don't correct him because you've had a bad day or because you are angry or frustrated. Overly rough or unfair corrections will not teach Champ and they are not effective or humane training techniques. Instead, if you are unfair or too rough, you will frighten Champ, teach him to distrust you or even to fight and possibly bite you.

Any correction, whether it is your voice, the leash or the squirt bottle, should be forceful enough to get Champ's attention and *no more.*

Whenever possible, follow every correction by showing Champ what to do. If he's on the furniture, take him to his blanket. If he's chewing on the kids' toys, take those away and give him one of his toys. Correct him for his mistakes and then show him what to do.

Interrupt Champ's Train of Thought

An interruption is not quite a correction —it's not as forceful—instead, an interruption tells your dog to stop whatever it is that he's doing, or what he's thinking about doing. If you can interrupt Champ as he sniffs the garbage can, you can make him understand that the trash can is off-limits. If you interrupt him as he starts to bark—as he makes his first "Woof!"—you can teach him that barking at the baby is not allowed. By interrupting him as he is starting to make a mistake, or better yet, as he is thinking about it, you can be a much more effective teacher.

As you are teaching Champ, watch his body language and see what he does and what he looks like as he thinks about things. What does he look like when he's getting ready to do something he's not supposed to do? Does he look to see where you are? Is his head down? Is he sniffing the air toward the trash can? Does he leave the room in a hurry? As you learn to read his body language and can tell when he's going to get into trouble, you can interrupt his train of thought: "Champ, don't even think about it. Come lay down. Good boy to lay down!" By doing this, you are telling your dog you are supernatural and telepathic—a great lesson for Champ to learn! You are also preventing problems from happening and you are praising your dog for doing something right.

An interruption can be your voice alone: "Hey! What are you doing?" It might also be your voice and a spray from the squirt bottle: "Be quiet!" Or it might be your voice and a snap and release of the leash, if Champ happens to be wearing it. Remember, an interruption should be forceful enough to get Champ's attention and no stronger.

Timing Is Everything

When Champ is doing something that is interesting to him, such as sniffing the grass or raiding the trash can, he isn't thinking about the past or the future. He is thinking about what is happening at that particular moment. Therefore, when you are teaching him, the timing of your praise, permissions, interruptions and corrections is extremely important.

Your praise should be given *as* Champ does something right. When you tell him to sit and his rump tou-ches the ground, praise him. When you tell him to be quiet and he does, praise him when he closes his mouth. The same goes with permissions, interruptions and corrections.

If you see Champ sniffing the trash can in the kitchen, give him a verbal interruption ("Acck! Leave it alone!") as he is sniffing, before he grabs something out of the can. By interrupting his sniffing, you are telling him, "I know what you're thinking. Don't do it!" If your response is too slow, even by a few seconds, you may be responding to something entirely different. Let's use the kitchen trash can again as an example. Champ is sniffing the trash can while you are talking to a friend on the telephone. You see Champ sniffing but don't want to interrupt your friend, so you wait a few seconds. When she stops to take a breath, you tell her, "Shirley, hold on a second." You then tell your dog, "Champ, leave it!" But in those few seconds Champ had already decided to leave the trash can alone and had picked up his toy. Hearing your command, he spits out his toy and looks at you, then his toy, then you, totally confused. A few seconds can make a big difference.

The Right Lesson

Make sure that you are teaching Champ what you want him to learn. For example, one day you open the gate to take out the trash cans and Champ dashes through the gate. He sees your neighbor's cat and starts to chase it. However, he stops chasing it and comes back to you when you call him. When he gets back to you, you start scolding him for dashing through the gate and chasing poor Snowball. However, that scolding isn't teaching Champ anything about the gate or the cat. Instead, that scolding is teaching Champ that when he comes back to you, he's going to get yelled at. Is that really what you want him to learn?

As you live with Champ, interact with him and teach him, try to keep in mind what you are telling him with your words and actions. Think about the world around you and Champ in very simplistic terms. Things are either right or wrong. Praise Champ when he is doing something right and give permission when he's about to do something right. Interrupt mistakes that are about to happen and correct mistakes as they happen.

Some Additional Training Tips

When you start training, practice the lessons at home or in the backyard. Champ is comfortable there and will be more likely to pay attention to you. Once he has learned the lesson, start taking him other places so that he learns that these new things apply elsewhere, too. Start by going out front, then down the block. Later, take him to a local park or schoolyard. Teach Champ that these new rules apply everywhere.

Keep your lessons short, at first maybe just five minutes. Then reward Champ for the training session by playing with him or cuddling him. As he gets better and develops more concentration, you can gradually increase his training sessions, but always stop on a high note; always finish with something positive.

You don't need to yell or scream at Champ, either when giving commands or when correcting him. Champ can hear very well. If Champ isn't paying attention, yelling isn't going to change anything. Instead, teach Champ to listen to you. Give commands in a normal tone of voice. Praise him when he pays attention. When you are interrupting Champ or correcting him, again, don't yell. Instead, be firm and sound intense.

You also have to mean what you say. If you correct Champ for something and then giggle, he's not going to take you seriously. You must mean what you say and believe in what you are doing.

Never try to train Champ when the pressures of your day will cause you to be angry or short with him. He didn't cause your bad day at work! Don't train Champ when you are angry or sick, or worse yet, when you are drunk or stoned.

Dog training requires fairness, patience, persistence and consistency. Champ didn't ask to be trained and when you begin training, he doesn't understand the new rules. Champ doesn't understand why the sit is so important to you. Nor does he know why he isn't allowed to raid the trash can. After all, there is food in there and if you aren't going to eat it, why can't he?

Show Champ what you want him to do; not just once, but many times. When he does it right, with your help, praise him. When he does it right by himself, really praise him!

CHAPTER 3

Start Your Puppy Right

© PAM POSEY-TANZEY '96

A young puppy is a blank slate, just waiting for you to give him instructions. What you write on that blank slate will have considerable impact on what your dog will grow up to be. Therefore, it's important that you keep a vision in your mind of this puppy as an adult. Is he going to weigh four pounds full grown or eighty pounds? Do you want him to grow up to be a companion and a jogging partner? Do you want to do therapy dog work with him later? Do you want him to be a playmate for your children? Visualize Champ full grown and well trained.

As he is growing and developing, keep these goals in mind so that you can teach him what is acceptable (and what is not) and so that those goals can be realized. Don't let him do anything as a puppy that will be unacceptable later.

Socialization

Even though dogs as a species have the innate ability to bond with mankind, the bond itself does not happen automatically. Each individual puppy must be socialized with people so that he can develop that bond. When you bring your new puppy home, you can continue this socialization by gradually introducing Champ to a variety of different people. Note the key word: gradually. Don't invite all your family members and the whole neighborhood in to see your new puppy on his first day home, but instead, after he has settled in, introduce Champ to one or two different people a day.

Many new puppy owners voice their concern that all of this socialization to other people will weaken the bond they want the puppy to develop with them, the new owner. Don't worry about it. First of all, you will be spending more time with Champ than anyone else. As you live with him, feed, care for and, most importantly, train him, the bond between you and your new puppy will grow strong.

When Champ visits with other people, make sure the visits are fun and happy. Don't let someone scare him, hurt him or startle him. Don't let anyone pull his ears, wrestle with him or play-fight with him. If Champ learns that some people pull his ears, or jump out from behind trash cans going "Boo!" he could have problems the rest of his life with certain people or situations. Keep visits upbeat, happy and controlled.

Household Rules

It's important to start establishing some household rules as soon as your new puppy joins your household. Champ, at eight or nine weeks of age, is not too young to learn. By starting young, you will be preventing bad habits from getting started.

When deciding what rules you want to establish, look at your puppy, not as the baby he is now but as the adult he will grow up to be. You may not mind if Champ is on your couch now, but are you still going to want him on the furniture when he is full grown and shedding? What about jumping on people? Do you want your dog jumping on the neighbor kids and your grandparents?

Some common household rules might include teaching Champ not to jump on people, to behave when guests come over, to leave the trash cans alone, to stay out of the kitchen and not to chew on inappropriate things. Additional rules might include leaving the kids' toys alone, not dragging out dirty clothes, staying off the furniture and not stealing food.

To teach Champ what is allowed and what is not, you must be very clear with your commands and corrections. You must be consistent with your training, and you need to provide alternatives. For example, if you want to teach Champ not to jump on you, teach him to sit. Sitting is the alternative action because he can't jump on you and sit at the same time. When Champ does try to jump, tell him, "No jump!" and help him into the sitting position. Then, when he's sitting, praise him.

If there are several people in the household interacting with the puppy, list the household rules you wish to establish and post them in a prominent spot, such as on the refrigerator. (Post them right next to Champ's new vocabulary list.) Make sure everyone agrees with the rules, understands why they are important and knows how to teach the puppy. Everyone must be consistent with the training, or Champ will never be reliable.

Social Handling

Champ cannot care for himself; you must be able to trim his nails, clean his ears, brush him and do everything else necessary to keep him clean and healthy. Unfortunately, Champ doesn't understand that trimming nails and cleaning ears are necessary, and he may struggle when you try to do these things. The social handling exercise will help teach Champ to accept your ministrations.

25

Kneel down on the floor and with your puppy in front of you, lift him slightly and turn him so that you can lay the puppy on his side, his feet away from you, on the floor in front of your knees. Give Champ a little tummy rub to help him relax. If he is really wiggling or struggling, gently restrain him with one hand as you stroke him with the other. Be firm and gentle with Champ.

When Champ is no longer struggling, start giving him a massage and at the same time, examine his body. Run your hand over his back, down the shoulders, down the hips and over the rib cage. Touch each ear, run your hands over his head and look at those sharp puppy teeth. Check each paw for cuts or scratches and touch each toenail. Touch every part of Champ's body.

26

If at any time during this exercise Champ struggles or fights you, stop the massage, restrain him firmly yet gently and use your voice to correct the puppy, "Acck! No fight!" When the puppy has relaxed again, speak soothingly to him, "That's very nice. Good boy."

Once Champ has learned to accept this handling and, hopefully, has come to enjoy it, you can use it while caring for him. While he is laying still, you can brush him, check for fleas or ticks, trim toenails, comb out burrs or matts, even medicate him, if you need to.

This social handling exercise can also be used to calm an excited puppy. If, for example, when you let Champ into the house from the backyard and he is bouncing all over, running up and down the halls and jumping all over the furniture, you have a couple of choices. If you try to correct Champ, you will probably just make him more excited. Instead, catch him and just lay him down in front of you, as described above, and start giving him a slow, gentle rubdown. You are calming and relaxing Champ while at the same time giving him the attention he wants and needs from you.

The social handling will also help when Champ needs to go to the veterinarian's office. If the veterinarian needs to check his ears, look at his teeth or examine him in any way, Champ will be used to being handled.

Accepting the Leash

All dogs need to become familiar with a leash and this can be very difficult for some puppies. If Champ is frightened by the leash, maybe when the leash first applies pressure on his neck, he may never willingly accept a leash or it may take him a long time to forget about that first scary experience. However, you can teach Champ that good things happen with the leash.

Soon after you bring Champ home, put a soft nylon or cotton buckle collar on him. Make sure it is loose enough to slip off should he get it caught on something. After a day or two, when he is no longer scratching at the collar, attach a leash to the collar and let him drag it around the house for ten or fifteen minutes, while you watch him to make sure it doesn't tangle on something. While Champ is dragging the leash, he will step on the leash, feel the tug on his neck and just generally get used to the feel of it.

After two or three sessions of dragging the leash, you can teach Champ to follow you when you have the leash in hand. Have a few pieces of a soft treat you know he likes, such as hot dog or cheese. Let him sniff the treat and

then back away from him while you verbally encourage him, "Champ, let's go! Follow me! Good boy!" When Champ follows you for a few feet, stop, praise him and let him have a bite of the treat.

Repeat the exercise two or three times and quit for this session. Reward Champ by giving him a tummy rub or throwing a toy. After two or three training sessions like this, start making it more challenging by backing away from Champ faster or by adding turns. If he balks or acts confused, use your voice and the treat to encourage him.

Never stop the training session because your puppy is upset, angry or confused. If you do, Champ will learn he can make you do what he wants—a bad lesson for any puppy to learn. Instead, always end the training session on a high note; stop when Champ has done something well.

Start Teaching the Come

The come is one of the most important commands you can teach Champ and it is also one of the easiest to teach. If you buy dog treats that come in a cardboard box, you have probably already noticed that Champ has learned what that box sounds like when you reach in to get a treat. You can use that to teach your puppy to come.

Find an empty, small plastic container with a lid, like a margarine container. Put a handful of dry dog food kibble in the container and shake it. It should make a nice rattling sound. Now, have a few treats in one hand that you know your puppy likes. Rattle the container, ask Champ, "Do you want a cookie?" and pop a treat in his mouth. Repeat this exercise several times a day for two or three days. When Champ comes dashing to you when you shake the container, you are ready to move on.

When you shake the container now, tell Champ, "Champ, come!" in the same happy tone of voice you use when you ask if he wants a cookie. Back away from him a few steps so that he does come to you, then reward him with verbal praise and a treat. When he is chasing you those few steps, start calling him across the room or out in the fenced backyard.

At this early point in training, do not try to call Champ outside of a secure area; Champ isn't ready for that yet. Also, continue popping the treat in his mouth when he comes to you. You want to use this sound stimulus and food reinforcement for several months; this is an important command.

Be Aware

As Champ grows and develops, many things that happen normally around the house can be giving him messages you may not be aware of. These can greatly affect your relationship with Champ. For example, if you have a two-story house, you may have noticed Champ dashing up the stairs ahead of you and then turning to watch you come up. You may think this is very innocent but it's not to him. Champ is savoring the fact that you are following behind with your eyes lowered as you climb the stairs. This puts him in the dominant (leader-of-the-pack) position. You can stop it by leashing Champ and making him follow you up the stairs. It's safer to have Champ follow you up the stairs, too; you won't trip over him if he's following you.

The same thing can happen when you go through a door. Does Champ dash through every doorway ahead of you? Again, the dominant dog goes first. Leash Champ or block his way with your leg and make him follow you.

Even something as necessary as feeding Champ can give him unwanted messages. First of all, you should always eat first. The dominant dog eats first, then the less dominant members of the pack eat. After you have eaten (even just an apple or a few carrot sticks), then feed Champ. Leave the food down for fifteen minutes and then pick up the bowl.

Don't leave it down all day or for hours at a time. Champ needs to learn that food doesn't appear on its own, but, instead, that you are the giver of food. House-training will also be much easier when food is eaten on a regular schedule rather than nibbled at all day.

Feeding Champ at a specific time will have additional benefits. If, some day, he is ill or injured, one of the first questions your veterinarian will ask is, "How is Champ's appetite? How much did he eat today?" Having the food down all day can also attract ants, roaches, birds or rodents, all of which can transmit diseases to Champ.

Patience and Consistency

Raising and training a puppy requires a great deal of effort from you. You must establish a household routine that will work for the both of you and you must adhere to that routine. You will, of course, love your puppy, yet you must also set up rules for the puppy to follow. You must be consistent with your training and you must be incredibly patient. It all pays off.

There is nothing in this world like the relationship you will have with this new puppy. Champ will love you with all his heart, following you, trying to climb in your lap or simply sitting by your side. And as Champ grows up, he will know you better than you know yourself and will love you no matter what your failings. It's a wonderful relationship.

CHAPTER 4

House-Training and Crate-Training

Mention the fact that you are house-training a new puppy and people will tell you the most amazing things. "Rub the puppy's nose in his mess." "Throw him outside after he's had an accident." "Make him live outside until he is six months old." "All puppies should be paper-trained." "Never paper-train a dog." With all of the conflicting advice, it's amazing that so many dogs eventually do become house-trained. However, house-training doesn't have to be mysterious or difficult.

The Denning Instinct and Crate-Training

By about five weeks of age, most puppies are starting to toddle away from their mom and littermates to relieve themselves. You can use this instinct, with the help of a crate, to help you house-train Champ.

A crate is a plastic or wire travel cage that you can use as Champ's bed. Many new puppy owners shudder at the thought of putting their new puppy in a cage. "I would never do that! It would be like putting my child in jail!" A puppy is not a child, however, and has different needs and instincts. Puppies like to curl up in small, close places. That's why they like to sleep under coffee tables or chairs. Plus, Champ's instinct to keep his bed clean and the sense of security he derives from the crate are useful tools for training.

Because few puppies will voluntarily soil their beds, the crate teaches Champ to hold his wastes for gradually increased periods of time, so he will gradually develop more bowel and bladder control. You are responsible for making sure that he is never left in the crate too long.

Because the crate will be Champ's den or bed, it will also become a place of refuge. If he is tired, allow him to go back to his crate to sleep. If he is

35

overstimulated or excited, put him in his crate to calm down. When he doesn't feel good, he will go back to his crate to hide. Because the crate also confines the puppy, it can prevent some unwanted behaviors, such as chewing on electrical cords or destroying slippers.

Introduce Champ to the crate by propping open the door and tossing a treat inside. As you do this, tell Champ, "Go to bed!" and let him go in to get the treat. Let him investigate the crate and go in and out freely.

When Champ will go in after a treat and has sniffed the crate thoroughly, offer a meal in the crate with the door still propped open. Because food is important, and because all puppies are motivated by their stomachs, feeding Champ in his crate helps him overcome any fears he might have.

Offer the next meal in the crate, and this time close the door once Champ is inside, but be prepared to open the door as soon as Champ discovers that the door is closed. The third meal can be fed with the door closed for five minutes. After the third meal, start feeding Champ in his normal place again, and simply offer him a treat or a toy for going into the crate. Continue teaching the phrase, "Go to bed!"

Don't let Champ out of the crate if he has a temper tantrum. If he starts to cry, whine, howl, bark or chew at the crate, correct him verbally, "Ack! Quiet!" or simply close the door and walk away. If you let him out when he makes a fuss, you will teach him that throwing a temper tantrum works. Instead, let him out when you are ready to let him out and only when he is quiet.

Put the crate in your room at night so that Champ can spend eight uninterrupted hours near you. Knowing that you are nearby will give him a feeling of security. Nighttime is a great time for bonding, too, so use your sleeping hours to benefit your relationship with Champ by keeping him close.

Don't exile Champ to the backyard, laundry room or garage at night. He will cry or whine with fear and loneliness and may develop destructive habits (such as chewing and tearing things apart) to try and cope with those emotions. In addition, if he is exiled at night, when he is with you he may become overly active and anxious because he wants to be with you so much more.

Having Champ's crate nearby will also save you some hassle. If he is lonely, restless or starts to whine, you can reach over and tap the top of the crate as you tell him to be quiet. If he needs to go outside, you will hear him fuss and can take him outside before he has an accident.

Good Teaching

One of the most common methods of house-training a puppy is paper-training. The puppy is taught to relieve itself on newspaper and then, at some point, is retrained to go outside. Paper-training, unfortunately, teaches the puppy to relieve itself in the house. Is that really what you want your puppy to learn?

Instead, teach Champ exactly what you want him to do. Take him outside to the area where you want him to relieve himself, and tell him "Go potty!" (Use any command comfortable to you.) When he has done what it is he needed to do, praise him, "Good boy to go potty!"

Don't just let the puppy out into the backyard and hope that he goes. You may let him back in the house just to see him squat on the rug. You have to go with him so that you know that he has gone and so that you can praise him for relieving himself.

If you try to train Champ by punishing him for accidents that happen in the house, either by rubbing his nose in his mess (a commonly used correction) or sharply scolding him, you will confuse Champ more than you will teach him. If you correct Champ severely for house-training accidents, he will start being sneaky about going potty. He won't allow you to watch at all, inside or outside, and he will sneak off to the back bedroom. Remember, the act of relieving himself is not a problem, it is relieving himself in the house that is the problem.

Successful teaching is based on setting Champ up for success. Don't allow any accidents to happen and praise him when he does relieve himself in the proper place outside.

Establish a Routine

All babies need a routine, and Champ is no different. House-training is much easier if there is a schedule for eating, eliminating, playing, walking and sleeping. A workable schedule might look like this:

6:30 a.m. Dad wakes up and takes Champ outside. After Champ relieves himself and is praised for doing so, Dad fixes Champ's breakfast, offers him water and then takes him back outside. Junior goes out and plays with Champ for a few minutes before getting ready for school.

7:30 a.m. Mom goes outside to play with Champ before getting ready for work. Just before she leaves, she brings Champ inside, puts him in his crate and gives him a treat.

11 a.m. A dog-loving neighbor comes over, lets Champ out of his crate and takes him outside to relieve himself. After praising Champ for going potty, she tosses the ball for him. When Champ has used up some excess energy, she sits down and cuddles the puppy for a few minutes, then takes him back to his crate and gives him a few treats.

3 p.m. Junior gets home from school and lets Champ out in the backyard. After Junior changes clothes, he and Champ go for a walk. When they come home, Junior leaves Champ in the backyard.

6 p.m. Mom brings Champ in and feeds him his dinner. When he has finished eating, she takes him back outside to relieve himself. After praising him for going potty, she brings him back inside to spend time with the rest of the family.

8 p.m. After Champ and Junior play in the living room, Mom has Junior take Champ back outside so that Champ has a chance to relieve himself. After he goes, Junior brings Champ back inside.

11 p.m. Dad takes Champ back outside for one last potty break, then brings him in and crates him for the night.

The schedule you establish will have to work with your household routine and your life-style. But keep a few things in mind. First, the puppy should not remain in its crate for longer than four hours at a time except at night. Second, Champ will need to relieve himself at some very specific times, including after eating or drinking, after exercise and when he wakes up from sleeping. Third, Champ needs some supervised activities with the family, both inside and outside, even if that means you need to schedule those activities.

Limit Champ's Freedom

The puppy who spends a great deal of time away from his family will have more difficulty learning to be part of the group, part of the family pack. Champ needs to be with the family during family activity time. If your family traditionally gathers in the dining room or family room in the evening, make sure Champ is included.

He can be loose in the room if someone can supervise him. A baby gate across the doorway will ensure that Champ doesn't sneak off to another room to have an "accident." If no one can watch him, bring his crate into the room with you and have him rest in his crate. Give him a toy to play with or something to chew on. Don't let Champ have too much freedom too soon.

Practice Patience

New puppy owners seem to invite advice. Everyone has a method of house-training that works better or faster and is more reliable than anyone else's method. Ignore your well-meaning friends. All puppies need time to grow up and develop bladder control. Establish a schedule and household routine that works for you and stick with it. If you keep changing schedules and techniques, you and Champ will both become frustrated and confused.

If you follow the schedule, Champ will progress. However, don't let his quick success go to your head; don't assume that he is house-trained. Too much freedom and too little supervision will result in problems. A schedule that is comfortable for you and Champ will work. When Champ has grown up, all your efforts will pay off when you have a well-house-trained, reliable dog.

CHAPTER 5

The Basic Obedience Commands

© PAM POSEP-TANZEY

A good obedience program is much more than just teaching your dog to sit and stay; instead, it is the foundation for your entire relationship. This relationship should be based on several factors. First, Champ should understand that he is living in your house, not you in his, and that you can establish some rules for him to follow. Plus, there should be mutual affection and respect between you and your dog.

Use lots of praise, petting and laughter when you train Champ. When he does something right, let him know that by using enthusiastic praise: "Yeah! Good dog! Super!" Keeping the training upbeat will help keep it fun, and you will find that both of you will enjoy your training sessions.

When you must correct your dog for inappropriate behavior, use fair but firm corrections—just enough to get your dog's attention. Don't use too much force, scream and shout or lose your temper. If you do, you will lose your dog's respect and possibly scare or intimidate him. As a result, you can seriously damage both your training and your relationship.

When you teach your dog the basic commands, you can also be teaching him the rules of your household. You can teach him not to jump on people and to sit at the doorway instead of dashing out ahead of you. Establish guidelines for behavior that will be comfortable for both you and your dog, and then stick to them.

Sit and Release

The sit is the most important foundation command for several reasons. First of all, when Champ learns to sit, he is learning to control his own actions, to hold still. He is also learning that if he does hold still, he will be praised. The sit is also a replacement action to help correct or prevent jumping on people; after all, your dog can't sit in front of you and jump on you at the same time. And finally, the sit is the foundation command for many other training exercises.

There are several different ways to teach your dog to sit. With the first method, have a treat in your hand and let Champ sniff it. As your dog sniffs it, slowly move your hand over his head, toward his tail. At the same time, take a small step toward your dog as you tell him, "Champ, sit." When his head goes up to follow the treat in your hand, he will probably sit because that will be more comfortable than craning his head backward. When he sits, praise him and give him a bite of the treat.

©PAM POSEY-TANZEY

If Champ sits but then pops back up when you praise him, use one hand to offer the treat and the other hand to rest on his collar to prevent him from popping back up. After praising your dog, pat him on the shoulder and tell him, "Okay, Champ." This release command, the pat on the shoulder and the word okay, tells Champ you are through and he can move.

If Champ is not sitting well for this method, perhaps spinning around after your hand instead of looking up, you can use your hands to shape him into the sit position. Again, tell him, "Champ, sit." As you do, put your right hand on the front of Champ's chest as your left hand slides down his back to the rump and gently shapes him into a sit. Again, praise him while he is sitting and do not allow him to pop up until you release him.

Don't get into the habit of repeating your commands. If you tell Champ to sit three, four or five times before making him do it, you are teaching him that he doesn't have to listen to you the first time. Instead, teach him that you expect him to respond to the first command.

There are a variety of ways you can use the sit to help you around the house. As was stated before, Champ cannot jump on you (or other people) and sit at the same time. Therefore, by teaching him to sit for praise, you are eliminating the need for him to jump. He can't knock his food bowl out of your hand if you teach him to sit while you fix his meals. The same goes for playtime; have Champ sit when he brings back his ball or toys, and don't take the ball or throw it for him until he sits.

Lay Down

The lay down exercise continues one of the lessons the sit exercise started, that of self-control. It is hard for many dogs to control themselves, but it's a lesson that all must learn. Teaching and practicing the lay down teaches Champ to lay down and be still.

Start with Champ in a sit. Rest one hand gently on his shoulders and have a treat in the other hand. Let him smell the treat and then tell him, "Champ, lay down" as you take the treat straight down to the ground in front of his paws. As he follows the treat down, use your hand on his shoulders to encourage him to lay down. Praise him, give him the treat, have him remain in the down position for a few seconds and then release him in the same manner as you did from the sit. Pat him on the shoulder and say, "Okay!"

If Champ watches the treat but does not follow it, simply position him into the lay down position by lifting his front legs and sliding them forward. The rest of the exercise is the same.

As Champ learns what lay down means, you can have him hold the position for a few seconds longer but do not step away from him. Stay next to him, and if you need to, keep a hand on his shoulder to encourage him to remain laying down.

Stay

When you taught Champ to sit, you taught him the sit position and to hold it for a few seconds until you released him. The same lesson was learned with the lay down; Champ was to lay down until you released him. The stay continues those exercises by teaching him to hold still for gradually increasing amounts of time as you walk away from him. Eventually, Champ will be able to hold the stay even when you walk into another room.

Start by having Champ sit. With the leash in your left hand, put a slight amount of pressure backwards (towards his tail) on the leash as you tell him to stay. At the same time, use your right hand to give Champ a signal that will mean stay—an open hand gesture with the palm toward his nose. Take one step away and at the same time release the pressure on the leash. If Champ moves toward you or lies down, tell him "Acck!" and put him back in a sit. Repeat the verbal stay command. After just a few seconds, step back to Champ and praise him enthusiastically, then release him.

You will use the same process to teach the stay in the lay down position. Have Champ sit, then lay down. With the leash in your left hand, put a little pressure back on the leash, tell Champ to stay, signal with the right hand and step away. Wait a few seconds, step back to the dog, praise him and release him.

With the stay command, you always want to go back to him to praise and release him. Don't release him from a distance or call him to you from the stay. If you do this, his stay will not be reliable; he will continue to get up from the position. When teaching Champ the stay, you want him to understand that when you say, "Stay!" he is to hold that position until you go back to him and release him. Period.

As Champ learns the command, you can increase the time he holds the stay. A four-month-old puppy could realistically hold a sit/stay for about thirty seconds and a down/stay for up to about a minute. A six-month-old puppy could double those times; an adult dog could hold the sit/stay for three to four minutes and the down/stay for up to a half an hour.

Use the down/stay to have Champ be still while you eat or visit with guests. Use either command to keep the dog still when you are talking to a neighbor. There are a lot of very practical uses for both commands; all you need to do is look at your normal household routine and see how they fit in.

The Come

The come is one of the most important commands you can teach your dog. In chapter 3, you learned how to teach your puppy to come using a shaker with treats in it. This is a good exercise for older puppies and adult dogs, too, for several reasons. First of all, most dogs like food, and using food as part of the training process increases their interest in the training. Second, by using a sound other than just your voice, it's easier to get your dog's attention. And third, when your dog comes when you call him and you give him a treat, you are teaching him that coming to you is very exciting and rewarding, which is a good message for him to learn.

Review the section on teaching the come in chapter 3. Continue training this way for quite a while—several months at the minimum. You can use this sound stimulus and food reinforcement for as long as you need to, at least while Champ is growing up; this is an important command.

There is a second way to teach the come. With this method, you will need a length of cotton clothesline rope. Don't use nylon; that will be too rough

on your hands. If you have a big dog, cut off a thirty- to forty-foot length of rope. If you have a smaller dog, cut it proportionately shorter. Fasten the rope to Champ's collar and let him go play. Watch him closely so that he doesn't get the rope tangled, of course, but let him do something other than pay attention to you. When he's distracted by his toys or smells in the grass, call him: "Champ, come!" If he does not immediately turn toward you, grab hold of the rope and give it a tug toward you. If he comes, praise him enthusiastically: "Good boy to come! Yeah!"

If he doesn't come to you, use the rope to make him come. Reel him in like a fish at the end of a fishing pole if you need to. Don't let him learn that he can ignore you when you call him. But even if you have to reel him in, you must still praise him for coming to you. Champ must always be praised for coming to you, even if he doesn't have a choice in the matter.

Remember, what you teach him now will have bearing on his future behavior. If some day he gets out the front gate and is running toward the street where a car is coming, you don't want Champ to think about whether or not he's going to come to you. You want him to pivot in his tracks and come back to you, running at full speed!

Watch Me and Heel

In chapter 3, Champ learned to accept the collar and leash, and how to follow you on the leash. If he isn't following you well yet, review that section and practice it some more. When Champ will willingly follow you as you are backing up, you can then turn (as you are walking) so that you and Champ both are facing forward. As with the follow, show Champ the treat, bringing the treat up toward your face as you tell him "Watch me." When he is looking at the treat and you, start walking forward as you tell him, "Good boy, Champ, heel!" You want Champ to learn that "watch me" means "look at me" and "heel" means "walk by my left side without pulling."

If Champ tries to dash ahead of you, simply back away from him as you did when you were teaching him to follow you. If he doesn't see you back away, give a little snap on the leash: "Wow! What happened? Watch me!" Stick the treat in front of his nose again and encourage him to pay attention to you.

Practice the heel by setting up a couple of trash cans in the driveway and have Champ heel with you as you walk a figure-eight pattern around the trash cans. Do the same thing with a few lawn chairs or the dining room chairs. When Champ's concentration is a little better, have him heel out front while the neighborhood kids are playing. "Watch me" and "heel" can get boring quickly; so gradually, as Champ gets better, increase the challenges. Use lots of verbal praise when Champ is working well and keep the training exciting and fun.

Heeling requires quite a bit of concentration on Champ's part. Keep your training sessions short and sweet, with lots of praise and treats.

Use it or Lose it!

The best way to make these training exercises work for you is to incorporate them into your daily routine. Champ needs to know that he is to sit, not just during his training sessions, but every time you tell him to sit.

You also need to continue to practice these commands even after Champ knows them. Reinforcement is necessary while Champ is growing up—not because Champ will forget the commands, but because he needs to be reminded regularly that he must continue to listen to you.

Patience and Consistency

Training a dog requires a great deal of effort from you. You must establish a household routine that will work for both of you, and you must adhere to that routine. You must be consistent with your training, and incredibly patient.

CHAPTER 6

It's Your House, Not Your Dog's!

M any dog owners act as though their dog owns the house. The dog goes anywhere he wants, never has a door shut in his face, and if it is, all he has to do is bark and someone will come running to open it. The dog sleeps anywhere he wants, even on the owner's bed, and then has the audacity to growl should the owner ask him to move. Although these owners may not realize it, they have given their dog the title to the house. Meanwhile, the owners earn the money and pay the bills. Hmm! Something's not right!

Dogs, like people, are social animals. We live in groups and rules are needed to maintain order. We may rebel sometimes (we've all exceeded the speed limit at one time or another!), but we also know that some rules are necessary.

Dogs need rules, too, and when they live together in a family pack, the dominant dogs (usually one bitch [female] and one dog [male]) set some rules that the subordinate dogs must observe. These rules help maintain order in the group. The dominant dogs always eat first and get the best bones or toys. The dominant dogs get the best sleeping places, go through doors first and decide what the group is going to do.

In my household of three dogs (and multiple other pets), Ursa is the dominant female (after me, of course!). If Dax, the younger, smaller subordinate bitch, steps out of bounds—perhaps by trying to take one of Ursa's toys—Ursa will correct her first by growling and curling her lip. Ursa will also stand on tiptoes and elevate the hair on her back and shoulders (the hackles) so that she looks bigger and taller. Depending on what Dax has done, Ursa might even stand over Dax, placing her chin on Dax's shoulder.

If Dax doesn't respond quickly enough or in an appropriately subordinate manner, then Ursa will grab Dax by the scruff of the neck and press her to the ground—sometimes quite roughly. At this point, Dax will pull back her lips in an exaggerated grin, will roll belly up and will bare her throat. Her body language shows Ursa that she has submitted to Ursa's dominance. Once she submits, Ursa will back off. There is never any blood shed or even fur pulled; it's actually quite calm and quick. Ursa doesn't hold any grudges, either; once a correction is over with, it's done.

When you bring home a dog, your family takes the place of the dog's family pack and someone must be in charge. If you don't assume leadership, then your dog will and it won't be a pretty sight! The dog who has assumed the dominant position in the family will growl when someone asks him to move, will snap (and possibly bite) when anything of his is touched, and will ignore any commands you give him unless, of course, it's something he wants to do anyway!

Obviously, you cannot do the same things that a dominant dog can do to teach your dog he is subordinate to you. You don't look like a dog, and if you tried to do what a dominant dog might do, your dog would laugh at you. However, you can adapt some things and make them work for you.

You Always Eat First

First of all, you should always eat first. Remember, the dominant dog always gets to eat first. If it's not time for one of your meals and you want to feed Champ, then at least eat an apple or a few carrot sticks. How much you eat is not important; it's the fact that you are eating that matters.

Take your dog, with his leash on, over to a spot in the dining room away from the table. That spot should be away from foot traffic so you won't trip over him. You can even put down a little throw rug, to give your dog a target. "Champ, this is your spot." Have your dog lay down and stay (see chapter 5). Place your meal (or snack) on the table and sit down to enjoy it. Should your dog move from the down stay, take him back to his spot, have him lay down, tell him stay again, and leave him. The first time you try this, your dog may break the down stay two dozen times. Don't give up; keep correcting him and taking him back to his original spot. If he holds the down stay, praise him enthusiastically! When you finish your meal, release him from the down stay and feed him his dinner.

Get Champ's Attention

If Champ likes to ignore you, teach him to pay attention to you. Hold a treat in one hand and let Champ smell it. Then tell him, "Champ, watch me!" and take the treat up to your face. He's going to watch and see what you're doing with the treat. When he looks at your face, praise him: "Good boy to watch me!" Then give him the treat.

The watch me will be very positive in the beginning because you're using treats. But you are also teaching him to look at you—to pay attention to you. Once he knows the command, you can tell him to watch you when he's distracted by something or when you want to give him another command.

Many dogs will behave nicely at home but act like wild animals when they are out in public. The "watch me" can help with this, too. Have him sit and tell him to watch you. It's very difficult for him to dance around like a

wild dog and at the same time pay attention to you. When he does pay attention to you and ignores distractions, praise him enthusiastically!

First Through Doorways

In the dog's language, the dominant dog is always first. To use this instinct, you need to go through all doorways first. Don't allow your dog to charge through ahead of you. To teach him, put your dog's leash and collar on and walk him up to a doorway. Tell him to sit and wait. Walk away from him to the doorway. If he tries to dash, use the leash to correct him and take him back to the spot where you left him. Then, after he has held the sit for a few seconds, tell him, "Champ, okay, follow me," and turn and walk through the doorway. Use the leash to make sure your dog follows you instead of dashing ahead of you. If he tries to dash past you, use the leash to restrain him or block him with your leg or body. Take him back inside the doorway and repeat the exercise.

When your dog is starting to understand, practice this at other doorways, especially doors to the outside. Teach your dog to wait at the front door, the garage door, the back door and the gate. When you teach him to wait for permission to go through a door, you are, at the same time, stopping him from dashing outside.

If you live in a house with stairs, teach this exercise on the stairs, too. Don't let Champ dash past you on the stairs and then turn around and stare down at you. Instead, make him wait for you.

Once you start training this exercise, make sure you give Champ permission to follow you through a doorway every time he is to walk through one. If you and Champ are going for a walk, stop at the front door, have Champ sit and hook up his leash, then when you are ready, open the door, step through and tell him, "Okay, Champ, follow me." If he assumes that he is going and dashes through without your permission, take him back inside, have him sit, and tell him "Champ, wait." After a few seconds, give him permission to follow you.

Sit for Everything

Almost all the breeds of dogs seen today were originally bred for a purpose. Newfoundlands are water rescue dogs, Australian Shepherds are herding dogs, Labrador Retrievers bring back birds shot by the hunters and Greater Swiss Mountain dogs pull heavy wagons. With all of these working instincts, many dogs have a strong desire to work, or if not to work, to do something, anything. Often this desire to do something results in destructive or problem behavior. These dogs might chew up the sofa, dig up the backyard or bark incessantly.

However, you can channel some of that desire to work by having Champ sit for everything he wants. Have Champ sit before you give him a treat, before you put down his food bowl, before you hook up his leash and even before you lean over to pet him. When Champ brings you his ball for you to throw, have him sit before you throw it. When you are relaxing in front of the television in the evening and Champ nudges your arm so that you will pet him, have him sit before you pet him. Have him sit for everything he wants.

Give Champ Permission

If you see Champ about to do something you approve of, perhaps laying down on his throw rug, tell him to do it, "Champ, go lay down." When he does it, praise him, "Good boy to go lay down!" Obviously, he was going to do it anyway, but this gives you the chance to tell him to do something and then to praise him for doing it.

Mean What You Say

Don't give Champ a command or direction unless you are ready to follow through and make him do it. If your arms are full of groceries, don't tell Champ to sit unless you are willing to put the groceries down, right away, and make Champ sit. If you are tired or busy when Champ wants to play, don't tell him to go lay down unless you will follow through and make sure he does it.

If Champ learns that you will repeat commands over and over, or that you won't follow through with a command, then he will learn that he can take his time deciding when to do it and when to ignore you. Not only is this annoying, but it could also be dangerous, especially if he decides not to come when you call him. When you give Champ a command, any command, make sure you follow through and make him do it.

Give Champ a Belly Rub

Once every day, invite Champ to roll over for a belly rub. After rubbing his tummy, start giving him a massage. Rub him slowly and gently, moving up and down his back, over the rib cage, around his ears and back down his chest. This is a wonderful way to spend time with your dog, to bond with him and to show him you love him. As you massage him, he will stretch, then relax, turning into canine mush. He might moan or groan, his eyes will close and his tongue will hang out of the side of his mouth.

After you have massaged him, while he's still relaxed, do any grooming that he might need. Brush him, check him for fleas or ticks and check his ears to see whether they need cleaning. Examine him for cuts, scrapes, bumps, lumps or bruises. Do everything you need to do to keep him clean and healthy.

Your Emotional Attitude

The leader is always confident. If you don't feel confident about your relationship with Champ, at least act like it! It's also important that you, as Champ's leader, be dependable and reliable. If you teach your dog that certain behavior is required, stick to that rule. Don't change your rules and requirements, or your dog will be thoroughly confused.

Many people want a dog to love, to cuddle and to pet. People also need to be needed and want their dog to need them. In many situations this works out just fine; however, sometimes a dog will take advantage of too much loving and petting. If Champ is young (less than two years of age) and is showing some attitude, then too much petting and coddling is not good for your emotional relationship. But that doesn't mean that you have to stop petting him. Instead, have Champ roll over for a belly rub when you want to pet him. Or have him sit before you pet him. This encourages him to work for your rewards rather than taking them for granted.

You Are Champ's Leader

We really don't know how dogs view the world; we can only guess. We are outside observers trying to piece together and understand what we can see. But since our dogs try so hard to fit into our world, it seems only fair that we should try to satisfy some of their needs, too. Their need for fair, consistent leadership is important, as are their needs for food, shelter, affection and company. Training is the way to provide your dog with the leadership he needs to be happy and well-adjusted.

CHAPTER 7

Does Your Dog Bark, Dig and Chew?

Very few dogs are intentionally bad. When Champ digs up your backyard, he's not saying to himself, "Ha! I'll get him for going off to work every day and leaving me here alone!" Even though you might believe that Champ is muttering under his breath, he really isn't. Unfortunately, though, the number one reason dogs are given up by their owners is because of problem behavior.

Unfortunately, most of the behavior that you might consider a problem—digging, barking, jumping on people, chewing and so on—aren't problems to Champ. Champ digs because the dirt smells good, because the weather is hot and he wants to lay in some cooler dirt or because you have gophers that he would like to catch. All of the things that you consider problems, Champ is doing for a reason.

However, that doesn't mean that there is nothing you can do. Most problem behavior can be worked with, and if it cannot be stopped entirely, it can be controlled or prevented.

What Can I Do?

Exercise

Exercise is just as important for Champ as it is for you. It works the body, uses up excess energy, relieves stress and clears the mind. How much exercise and what type depends on Champ. A fast-paced walk might be enough exercise for an adult Basset Hound, but a healthy Labrador Retriever will need a good long run or a fast-paced game of ball.

If Champ has some physical limitations or if you have any doubts about his exercise needs, talk to your veterinarian. When you start an exercise program, start gradually, especially if Champ has been a couch potato. Sore muscles are no fun.

Play

Play is different from exercise, although exercise can be play. Laughter is very much a part of play and that is what makes it so special. Researchers know that laughter is wonderful medicine—it makes you feel better—and because of that, it has a special place in your relationship with Champ. If training is sometimes difficult, and Champ is being destructive or getting into trouble, make time to play with him. Play is a great stress reliever, both for you and for Champ.

Sometimes dogs will intentionally get into trouble because they feel ignored. To some dogs, negative attention (corrections, yelling and screaming) is better than no attention at all. By setting some time aside just for Champ, you can avoid some of these situations.

Nutrition

Nutrition plays an important part in problem behavior. If Champ is not eating a good-quality food, or if he isn't digesting his food properly, his body may be missing some vital nutrients. If Champ is chewing on rocks or wood, is eating the stucco off the side of your house, grazes on the plants in your backyard or is eating dirt, he may have a nutritional problem.

Some dogs also need more than a dry kibble dog food. Many dogs eat greens, vegetables and even fruits. Keep in mind that wild canids eat not only the animals they have hunted, but the food that those animals ate. Wild canids are also opportunists, eating whatever is available, including fallen fruits.

Sometimes the premium-brand dog foods, the "better" dog foods, are too rich. Some dogs develop a type of hyperactivity when they eat a high-calorie, high-fat, high-protein dog food. Other dogs have food allergies that might show up as behavior problems.

If you have any questions about your dog's behavior in relation to food, or about the food you are feeding your dog, ask your veterinarian.

Health Problems

Some experts feel that twenty percent of all behavior problems commonly seen are caused by health-related problems. Sometimes thyroid problems can cause a behavior problem; so can hyperactivity, hormone imbalances and a variety of other health problems. Some veterinary experts have found a relationship between seizure disorders and unpredictable, aggressive behavior. If you have some concerns as to Champ's physical health, make an appointment with your veterinarian.

Training

Training can play a big part in controlling problem behavior. A fair yet firm training program teaches Champ that you are in charge, that he is below you in the family hierarchy. Training will reinforce his concept of you as a kind, calm, caring leader.

You can also use your training skills to teach Champ what is acceptable and what is not. To teach Champ, praise him or correct him (whichever is appropriate) as the behavior is happening, just as you did with the basic obedience commands. That means if you come home from work and find that Champ has dug up your garden, it is too late to correct him. You have to correct him as the dirt is flying.

Many dog owners have said, "Oh, he knows what he's done because when I come home he looks guilty!" No, Champ doesn't know that at all. Instead, Champ knows from experience that when you come home, he's going to get into trouble. You are going to yell at him for something! He's dreading you coming home. Is that what you want him to learn?

To teach Champ that you don't want him to dig, you need to catch him in the act and correct him as he is making the mistake. Then (and only then) will he understand what you consider wrong.

Prevent Problems From Happening

Because so many of the things we consider problems are not problems to Champ, to teach Champ, you need to prevent them from happening as much as possible when you are not there. If Champ finds out how much fun it is to chew up your sofa cushion, you may have a difficult time stopping him. The same applies to the kitchen trash can that is full of scraps (treasures to Champ!), the fruit trees in the backyard and the children's toys. It's much easier to prevent a problem from happening than it is to break a bad habit.

Preventing a problem from happening might require you to fence off the garden, build some new, higher shelves in the garage or maybe even build Champ a new dog run. Don't let Champ have free run of the house if he's getting into trouble. You may even need to institute some new household rules for you and other family members. Champ can't raid the trash cans if you take the trash cans out before they are overflowing and put the trash cans away before you leave the house. Champ will get into less trouble if everyone would close closet doors, pick up dirty laundry and put away their toys.

Part of preventing problems from happening involves limiting Champ's freedom. A young puppy or an untrained dog should never have unsupervised free run of the house; there is just too much he can get into. Instead, keep him in the room with you either by watching him, or better yet, by using baby gates across the doorways. If you can't keep him with you, put him in his crate or outside in his yard.

Dealing with Specific Problems

Digging, Uprooting Plants and Destroying the Garden

If your backyard looks like a military artillery range, you need to concentrate first on preventing these things from happening when you are not there to supervise Champ. If you come home eight hours later and try to correct Champ for the hole he dug when you left for work, you are wasting your time; your correction is much too late. Instead of understanding that he is being corrected for digging, Champ is going to think he's being corrected for you coming home.

Build Champ a dog run. Make the run big enough that Champ can move around and trot back and forth. Make sure there is shade, unspillable water and shelter from bad weather. When you leave him in the run, give him a toy and a treat, and put a radio in the nearest window, tuned to a soft, easy-listening station.

Then when you are home, let Champ out for supervised runs in the backyard. When he starts to get into trouble, you can interrupt his actions and teach him what is acceptable and what is not.

The destructive dog also needs exercise, training and play times every day to use up energy, stimulate his mind and spend time with you. Some dogs who habitually raid the garden crave fruits or greens. When you give Champ a treat, offer him a carrot or a slice of apple. Most importantly, don't let the landscape artist watch you garden; if you do, Champ will come to you later with all of those bulbs you planted earlier!

The Barker

Are your neighbors complaining because Champ serenades the neighborhood while you're at work? Or does he bark when people walk down the sidewalk? Dogs bark for the same reasons we talk; to communicate. Champ might be trying to tell you (or the world at large) that he is bored and lonely, or that someone is infringing on his territory. He might be barking because other dogs in the neighborhood are barking. There are lots of reasons why. So what can you do?

Start by teaching Champ to be quiet while you're at home. The squirt bottle (see chapter 2) works very well. Fill the bottle with water and add enough vinegar to make the water smell bad. (If you can smell the vinegar, Champ's sensitive nose will smell it even better!) When Champ starts barking, tell him "Quiet!" and squirt the bottle toward him so that he gets a good

whiff of the vinegar. When he stops barking to sneeze or rub off the vinegar, praise him: "Good boy to be quiet!"

When he understands what you want, go for a short walk outside. Listen and when you hear Champ barking, come back and correct him using the same technique. After a few corrections, when Champ seems to have the idea, ask your neighbor to help you. Go outside, leaving Champ in the house, and have your neighbor come out and talk. Maybe the kids can play and create a distraction. When Champ barks, run inside as fast as you can and correct him again. Repeat as often as you need until Champ understands.

Some dogs learn very quickly and will not bark when they know you are at home. If Champ is one of these dogs, you will have to be sneaky. Go through the motions of leaving, as far as changing clothes, grabbing your purse or briefcase (don't forget the squirt bottle!), and drive away. Park several houses away and very quietly walk back. Wait out in front of your neighbor's house. When you hear Champ start to bark, run home and correct him.

If Champ is still on to you, and simply will not bark when you're setting him up, then you may have to resort to one of the bark control collars. There are several on the market that are humane and effective. All are triggered by the dog's barking and administer a correction or deterrent to the dog. Some collars make a high-pitched sound, one squirts a whiff of citronella and others administer an electric shock. I do not recommend the shock treatment for most dogs; many will panic when corrected this way. However, the first two collars are quite effective with many dogs.

Some dogs will stop barking as you leave if you make leaving home very low-key and unexciting. A distraction also works well for many dogs. Take a small, brown, paper lunch bag and put a couple of treats in it. Maybe a dog biscuit, a piece of carrot, a slice of apple and a small toy. Tape the top shut and rip a very tiny hole in the side of the bag. As you walk out the door or the gate, give this to Champ. He will be so busy trying to figure out what's inside that he won't pay attention to you leaving.

Dashing Through Doors and Gates

This is actually one of the easiest problems to correct. Teach Champ to sit and stay at all doors and gates, and to hold that stay until you give him permission to go through and release him after you have closed the door. By teaching him that doors and gates are boundaries that require permission, you will eliminate the problem.

Start with Champ on a leash and walk him up to the door. Have him sit, tell him to stay and then with the leash firmly grasped in your hand, open the door wide and stand aside. If he dashes forward, correct him for breaking his stay: "Acck! No, stay!" Take him back where he started and do it again. If he continues to do it, give him a snap and release of the leash and collar as you correct him verbally. When he will hold the stay at this door, go to other doors and gates and teach the same lesson, the same way.

If Champ tries to sneak past you when he is not on the leash, block him with your leg or close the door in his face as you give him a verbal correction: "Acck! No!"

If Champ does make it outside, don't chase him. If you chase him it becomes a game. Use your shaker to call Champ to you, "Champ, do you want a cookie? Come! Good boy!" When you do catch him or he comes back to you, don't correct him. If you do, he learns that coming back to you results in a correction. Instead, praise him for coming to you.

Jumping on People

Champ can't jump on you or other people if he's sitting; it's physically impossible to do both of those things at the same time. Since Champ jumps on people for attention, if you teach Champ to sit when you pet him, you can eliminate the jumping.

When you come home from work and Champ is excited to see you, don't try to greet him with your arms full. Instead, greet him with empty hands. Then, when he tries to jump, grab him by the collar or the scruff of the neck and tell him to sit. When he sits, praise him, "Good boy to sit!" and pet him. If he tries to jump up again, use your hands to put him back into the sitting position.

If Champ is really excited and it's very hard for him to control himself, once he's sitting, roll him over onto his back and give him a belly rub and a massage.

You can also use the leash to teach Champ not to jump. When you are out for a walk and see your neighbor, don't let your neighbor pet Champ until you make Champ sit. If Champ starts to jump on your neighbor, use a snap and release of the leash and a verbal correction: "Acck! No jump! Champ, sit."

When guests come to your house, don't let them in until you leash Champ. You can ask them to wait a minute: "Hold on! I'll be right there. Let me leash Champ." When you let them in, again, don't let them pet Champ until he's sitting. If he is too excited and won't hold the sit, ask your guests to ignore Champ while you try to make him behave. They can pet him later when he's calmed down.

The key to correcting jumping on people is to make sure that the bad behavior is not rewarded. If someone pets Champ when he jumps up, the bad behavior is rewarded. When he learns that he gets all of the attention when he's sitting, then he will start sitting automatically for petting. When he does, praise him enthusiastically!

Other Problems?

Many behavior problems can be solved, or at least controlled, by using similar techniques. Try to figure out why Champ is doing this, what you can do to prevent the problem from happening and what you can do to use your training skills to teach Champ. Remember that a correction alone will not solve the problem; you need to prevent the problem as much as possible and also teach Champ what he can do.

If you still have some unresolved problems or if your dog is showing aggressive tendencies, contact your local dog trainer or behaviorist for expert help.

CHAPTER 8

Games to Play with Your Dog

©PAM POSEY-TANZEY

L ife with a dog is a constant learning process. Throughout your dog's life, you will be seeing and discovering new aspects of your dog. It's fun to watch Champ discover new things or learn to solve problems. A friend of mine taught her Welsh Terrier to recognize and distinguish three colors: yellow, red and blue. Many experts told her it couldn't be done, but she did it because she knew her dog was intelligent enough to understand what she was teaching her to do. Dog owners are limited only by their ability to communicate with and teach their dog.

But the thrill of discovery is not one-sided; your dog is constantly learning from you, too. As you have learned in previous chapters, Champ is constantly reading your body language, and many of the things you do with him tell him something about you.

The games you play with your dog can teach him something, too. Some games challenge your dog's intellect; some make him solve problems; some stimulate him into using some of his natural abilities. Hide-and-seek games teach your dog to use his scenting abilities to find someone or something. Name games teach your dog to identify people and things by name. Retrieving games are great for exercise and using natural retrieving skills.

Other games teach messages you might not want to teach your dog. Tug of war games teach your dog to use his strength against you. That's not a problem if you have a seven-pound Papillon, but it could be a problem if you have a seventy-pound Labrador Retriever. Tug-of-war games are great for building the confidence of a submissive dog but are not a good idea for a challenging, more dominant personality.

Wrestling is another game that many dogs like and enjoy but is not always a good idea, unless Champ has a very submissive personality that needs bolstering. If Champ is a normal young dog, full of life and ready to play, wrestling is not a good idea. It teaches Champ that he can use his strength against you, that you have no protection against his nails, teeth or body weight, and that he is much faster than you.

Puppies wrestle with each other in the litter all the time and it teaches them social rules. If one puppy is too rough, the other will yelp and cry and the aggressor will back off. However, most littermates are pretty much evenly matched. People, however, are not built to match a young, healthy dog that wants to wrestle. Eventually, Champ is going to start thinking he's bigger, stronger, faster and better than you.

Instead of playing games that could potentially threaten your relationship with Champ, play some games that give him more positive messages about you and challenge his abilities.

The Name Game

The name game is a great way to make Champ think. And don't doubt for a minute that Champ can think; he is capable of learning the names of many different items and people. Not only is this a great game for Champ, but it can come in handy around the house. Tell Champ to find your keys or your shoes. Send Champ after the remote control to the television, or to go find Dad. Plus, it's great fun to show off to your friends!

Start with two items that are very different, perhaps a tennis ball and a magazine. Sit on the floor with Champ and those two items, and have some treats that Champ likes. Tell Champ, "Where's the ball?" and bounce the ball so that he tries to grab it, or at least pays attention to it. When he touches it, tell him, "Good boy to find the ball!" and give him a treat.

When he is responding to the ball, lay it on the floor next to the magazine and send him after it. Praise and reward him for getting it. Now set several different items out with the magazine and ball, and send him again. When he brings back the ball, praise and reward him. When he is doing that well, place one of his toys out there, too, and send him. If he goes for his other toy, take it away, with no comment, and send him after the ball again. This is a critical step in his learning process and you may need to repeat it several times.

When he will pick up his ball from among several different items, including other toys, then start hiding the ball. Make it simple to start, maybe just partially hidden under a magazine. As he gets better, start making it more challenging.

When you can hide the tennis ball and Champ can find it, start teaching him the names of other items, following the same process. You will find that the first three items will be the most difficult. At this point Champ is learning the concept you are trying to teach him, and he is also learning how to learn. Once he understands that each of these things has a different sound, and that he needs to listen to you say those sounds, he will start learning much faster.

Care Bear, an Australian Shepherd, can identify and point out over a hundred different items, ranging from family members to toys, other dogs, different family cars and household items. Although Care Bear is a very intelligent dog, he is not that different from other dogs. Your dog has the same learning abilities and is limited only by your ability to teach him.

Hide-and-Seek

Hide-and-seek is a fun game, much like the hide-and-seek you played as a child, except that you (or other family members) will hide and Champ will find you. Champ will be much better at finding than you ever were, though, because he has such a sensitive nose and outstanding scenting abilities.

Start by teaching a family member's name (or your own) using the techniques you learned in the name game. When Champ can identify a family member, ask that family member to hide. Give that family member a treat for Champ and have him show Champ that he has one. Hold Champ as that family member goes and hides in a fairly easy location. Tell Champ, "Go find Junior!" and let Champ go. If he starts to look around and sniff, just be quiet and let him work and think. If Champ starts to look flustered or confused, tell him again, "Go find Junior!" and help him find him. When he goes to Junior, praise him enthusiastically and let Junior give Champ the treat.

As Champ gets better at this game, you can start making it more challenging. Have Junior hide in more difficult places or slightly farther away from Champ. Junior can also run around a little before he finds a hiding place, so that he leaves a more challenging trail. As Champ gets better, you can also cover his eyes so that he can't see Junior leave.

When Champ has learned the names of different family members and knows how to find them, you can use this skill around the house. Send Champ out to the yard to get the kids when it's dinnertime. Or have Champ take the *TV Guide* to Dad when he asks for it. Hide-and-seek is a lot of fun, is challenging for Champ and uses his natural scenting abilities.

Retrieving

Some dogs are born retrievers, willing and able to bring back anything that moves or is thrown. Some dogs like to chase things but don't always bring them back. Other dogs convey the impression that retrieving is awful and nothing belongs in their mouths except food. Some of these dogs can be taught that retrieving is fun, although some are never convinced.

If Champ likes to retrieve, all you need to do is fine-tune the game so that he brings the item all the way back to you and gives it to you without playing tug-of-war. If Champ hesitates on the way back, simply call him to you. If he drops the item, send him back to it, again using encouragement to have him pick it up and bring it to you. Don't scold him or try to correct him; that will only serve to discourage him.

If Champ likes to take the thrown item and run with it, playing keep-away, you have two options. You can stop the game and go inside, leaving Champ alone. This shows him that you will not chase him and the game will end when he tries to play keep-away. Or you can have a long leash (a length of clothesline rope) on Champ when you start the game so that if he tries to play keep-away, you can step on the rope, stop him, and use the rope to bring him back to you. If you need to use the rope, you still must praise Champ for coming back to you even if you made him do it. As you saw in chapters 3 and 5, the come must be positive.

If Champ doesn't like to retrieve, teaching it so that Champ enjoys it can sometimes be a long process, but you can do it and Champ can learn to like retrieving games. Ursa, as a puppy, hated to retrieve. However, she learned to retrieve using the method outlined below and now is an enthusiastic retriever, able and willing to chase anything and bring it back.

Start by sitting down on the floor and inviting Champ to lay down or sit in front of you. Have one of Champ's favorite toys and some good treats. Show Champ the toy, holding it in front of him. Tell him, "Champ, take it." If Champ sniffs or touches it, praise him and give him a treat. Do it again. When Champ will touch the toy as soon as you hold it up or give him the command, then you make the criteria harder. Now you want him to lick the toy or open his mouth before you will give him the treat and praise. When Champ will open his mouth, the next criteria is to open his mouth and put it around the toy. After that, start moving the toy, either in your hand or by tossing it just a foot or two. Use the same techniques and gradually build his skills until he is actually chasing the toy.

The key to this type of training is to be very patient and to not go on to the next step until Champ understands what you expect of him. If you rush this training, Champ will get very confused. However, once Champ can retrieve this toy and understands the concept and the commands, learning to retrieve other items will be very easy.

The Come Game

In this game, two family members will stand or sit across the room or yard from each other. Each will have a shaker (see chapter 3) and some treats for Champ. Taking turns, each will shake the shaker, call Champ to come and when he does, praise and reward him. This is a very simple game but it gives you a chance to practice the come command and makes it fun at the same time. Plus, everyone in the family can practice it, giving even the kids a chance to help train Champ.

The Shell Game

Do you remember seeing the shell game in old movies? A con man would put a ball or other object under an inverted bowl and then move that bowl and several others so that they were all mixed up. Someone then needed to choose the right bowl that was hiding the ball. You can play that game with Champ. The only difference is once he knows the game, he will win just about every time!

You will need three bowls of the same size and a handful of dog biscuits. Sit on the floor and have Champ watch you. Turn the bowls over and place a biscuit under one of the upside-down bowls. Tell Champ, "Find the biscuit!" If he finds it right away, praise him and give him the biscuit. If he doesn't understand, help him. Tilt the bowl a little so he can smell the biscuit.

When he has won the game a few times, make it more challenging. Hide the biscuit and then move the bowls around so that Champ can't tell (by sight) which bowl is hiding the biscuit. You can also make it more challenging by adding one or two more bowls.

Trick Training

Trick training is a lot of fun. It's a great way to improve your dog-training skills and a fun way for your dog to learn. Trick training is also entertaining;

therapy dogs use tricks to make people laugh all the time. Years ago, I taught one of our German Shepherd Dogs to play dead. Michi was so good at this trick, he could pick up the phrase "dead dog" out of a conversation; I didn't have to emphasize the command. Well, one of our neighbors graduated from the police academy and was very proud of his new uniform and badge. While I was out front talking to him, with Michi on a leash by my side, I congratulated my neighbor and then turned to Michi and asked him, "Michi, would you rather be a cop or a dead dog?" Michi dropped to the ground as if shot, rolled over on his side and closed his eyes. My neighbor was sputtering and turning red in the face, his wife was laughing so hard tears were running down her face and I was trying very hard not to laugh myself! It was wonderful!

Dead Dog

The goal of the dead dog trick is that Champ will lay on his side or back, become absolutely still and, if possible, close his eyes. Start by teaching him that dead dog also means lay down. He knows the down command, so have him lay down as you tell him, "Champ, lay down! Dead dog! Good boy!" After a few days of practice, reverse the commands: "Champ, dead dog! Lay down! Good boy!" When he is starting to lay down on the words dead dog, stop saying lay down.

Next, teach him that dead dog means more than simply lay down. Using your hands, very gently show him that you want him to lay his head down and be still. At first, only ask him to do this for a very few seconds, then praise him enthusiastically! As he shows that he understands, ask him to hold it longer.

When Champ will lay down on the dead dog command and will lay still, close his eyes by gently putting your hand over his eyes. Do this for just a second to start. If Champ is concerned about closing his eyes, talk to him as you do it. When he will close his eyes, praise him enthusiastically.

You will notice that as Champ understands what you want and as you praise him, he will start adding flourishes to the trick. Some dogs will drop to the ground so fast it's amazing they don't hurt themselves. Ursa lays down but then rolls over on her back, baring her belly, and then barks as if she's dying in excruciating pain! If you like his flourishes, simply praise them. Personally, I enjoy seeing what my dogs can add to our trick-training routines. I enjoy their creativity and imagination.

Shake Hands and Wave

Ask Champ to sit in front of you. Tell him, "Champ, shake," as you reach down and tickle his leg right behind his paw. He will lift his paw to get away from this annoyance and as he does, shake his paw and praise him, "Good boy to shake!" When he starts to lift his paw as you reach for it, stop tickling and simply praise him for shaking.

The wave is an extension of the shake. When he lifts his paw to shake, tell him "Wave," and reach for his paw but don't touch it. He will offer his paw again, not understanding this new trick. As he lifts his paw, praise him, "Good boy to wave." By withdrawing your hand (not letting him touch it) and lifting your hand, you can teach Champ to wave higher and longer. Make sure you reward his efforts.

Crawl

Have Champ lay down. With a treat in your right hand, move it from Champ's nose forward as you tell him, "Champ, crawl!" Lead him slowly with the treat. Your left hand can rest gently on his shoulders so that if he tries to get up to follow the treat, you can keep him down. After he has crawled a few steps, let him have the treat and praise him. As he learns the command, you can ask him to crawl longer distances. Once he learns the command, Champ will be able to crawl from your verbal command or from the hand signal, the hand moving forward from his nose.

Roll Over

Have Champ lay down. With a treat in one hand, tell him "Champ, roll over!" as you make a circle with the treat directly in front of his nose. With your other hand, roll him over. Make sure you are rolling him in the same direction that you are signaling with the treat. Once he understands, have him roll over once, twice or even three times in a row. As he learns the trick, you will be able to tell him to roll over with a verbal command or with the hand signal, a circle in front of his nose.

You can also teach him to roll over the other direction. If roll to the right is "Roll over!" then rolling to the left can be "Roll back!" Teach it the same way, signaling in the direction you want him to roll as you teach him the new command, and help him do it. If he rolls in the direction he is used to going, don't correct him or scold him. Do it again and show him what you want him to do.

Spin

Have Champ stand in front of you. Tell him, "Champ, spin!" as you take a treat from his nose to his tail and back up to his nose again. Draw a big circle over the top of your dog so that he follows the treat and turns in a big circle just as if he were chasing his tail. Make the signal with the treat slowly at first until he understands. When he will spin on command, add two or three spins so that he will do several circles. Don't do too many, though, or he may make himself dizzy or sick. When Champ is spinning on command and knows the trick well, you will be able to use either the verbal command, "Champ, spin!" or the hand signal to have him spin.

Jump

Start by teaching Champ to jump over something on command. A dowel or small stick works well. Hold the stick in front of Champ at about half his height and tell him, "Champ, jump!" as you encourage him forward. When he jumps, praise him. Practice by having him jump the stick at different heights, at different angles (tilted or slanted) and when he's walking or running. When he understands the command "Jump" and will willingly jump over the dowel, start having him jump other things so that he learns the word "Jump" means to jump rather than jump only the dowel.

When Champ will jump over something whenever you tell him to, kneel down, stick out one leg and ask him to jump over your extended leg. When he will do that, stick out one arm (at a reasonable height) and ask him to jump over your arm. Then make a circle with your arms and ask him to jump through your arms just like the tigers in the circus do.

If you have more than one dog, have one dog do a stand stay and have the second dog jump over the first dog's back. I can stand Ursa and have Dax jump over her. Dax thinks that's more fun than treats!

Dance

With Champ standing in front of you, tell him, "Champ, dance!" as you let him sniff a treat in your hand. Raise your hand over his head and encourage him to jump up and stand on his back legs for the treat. When he stands up, give him the treat and praise him. When he will readily jump up for the treat, move your hand so that he will bounce around a little as you tell him, "Champ, dance!" Praise him enthusiastically! Increase the amount of dancing very gradually. It takes time to build up those dancing muscles!

And there's more! Trick training can be a lot of fun and there's no limit to what you can teach your dog. What do you think is fun? How can you teach Champ to do it?

Any Others?

You can invent all kinds of games to play with Champ. Just think about the games before you teach him. What will Champ learn from this game? Is it something you really want him to know?

CHAPTER 9

The Next Step in Training

One of the great things about dog training is that you are never finished; there is always more you can teach your dog. Would you like Champ to behave himself off leash? You can teach him that. Wouldn't it be fun to teach Champ to recognize and respond to some hand signals? It is. Champ can learn hand signals for lay down, sit, stand, stay and more, including the directions left and right.

Some people teach advanced obedience commands for competition or other dog sports, which we'll talk more about in the next chapter, but some of these commands are great for your daily life with Champ. For example, if Champ responds to hand signals, you can give him the signal to go lay down and stay while you are talking on the telephone. That way you won't have to interrupt your conversation.

Before you start teaching Champ any of these commands, make sure Champ is proficient at his basic commands. He should be able to respond to the sit, down, stay and heel (on leash) with one command and very few corrections. Ideally, he should also come to you when you call (off leash in the house or fenced yard) using the shaker and a verbal command. If Champ is still having some trouble with the basics, work on those some more before going on to these commands.

Hand Signals

When you start teaching Champ hand signals, use a treat in your hand to get Champ's attention and use a verbal command to help him understand what you want. As Champ responds better and starts to show some understanding of the command, you can then make the verbal command softer, and eventually stop saying it.

The difficult part of teaching Champ hand signals is that in the beginning, Champ may not understand that there is some significance in your motions. After all, people move their hands constantly, especially when they are talking, and Champ may not realize that those motions could mean something. Also, for hand signals to work, Champ must be watching you!

Lay Down

When you taught Champ to lay down by taking a treat to the ground in front of his feet, you were starting to teach Champ a hand signal. Granted, he was watching the treat in your hand, but he was also getting used to seeing your hand take the treat there. That motion of your hand is a signal—a command that can mean the same thing as your verbal command "Lay down." Continue using the treat in the beginning; don't get rid of the treat until you are sure that Champ knows the signal and is following it reliably.

Start teaching Champ by practicing the lay down with the signal as you taught him in chapter 5. Have him sit, tell him "Lay down" and take the treat to the ground in front of him. When he's down, praise him and release him. If he's doing this well, with no hesitation, give him the signal and delay your whispered verbal command by a couple of seconds. If Champ lays down for your signal, praise him enthusiastically! If he waits for your verbal command, try it again with more emphasis on the signal.

When he can follow the signal with no verbal command, start making it more challenging. Continue to have Champ sit, but stand in front of Champ and signal him to lay down. Walk a leash length away and try it. Try it from across the room. Remember to praise him enthusiastically when he follows your signal and lays down.

Sit

If you were able to teach Champ to sit using the treat above his nose (see chapter 5), you were starting to teach him a signal that means sit. If you weren't able to use that technique, don't worry; he can still learn a sit signal.

With Champ on the leash held in your left hand, have a treat in your right hand, and standing in front of Champ, take the treat from his nose up to your left shoulder so that your forearm is a diagonal across your chest. At the same time, tell him, "Champ, sit" in a soft voice. If he hesitates, give him a jiggle of the leash and collar. If he refuses, tell him to sit again and snap and release the leash. When he sits, praise him, give him the treat, release him and try it again.

Stay

As you taught Champ the stay command earlier, you were again introducing him to a hand signal. When you said "Champ, stay" and put your open-palmed hand in front of his nose, that was a hand signal. In fact, this signal is so obvious, Champ will probably pick it up right away with little extra training. Try it by having Champ sit, then give him the stay signal without a verbal command and see what happens. Did he hold it? If he did, go back to him and praise him. If he didn't, put him back where he started, give him the signal again, and quietly tell him to stay.

Come

The come signal will start with your right hand and arm straight out to your side at shoulder height. Bring it around to your chest as if you were reaching out to get your dog and bringing him to you. Finish it by making the sit signal—the diagonal across your chest—so that when Champ comes dashing to you, he will see the sit signal and sit in front of you.

Start teaching it by having the come shaker in your right hand and shake it slightly as you make the arm signal and quietly tell your dog to come. You may also need to quietly tell your dog to sit as you finish with the sit command. Champ isn't used to watching more than one command at a time. When he comes and sits, praise him enthusiastically and give him a treat.

Watch Champ and when he seems to understand the signal, take away the shaker and practice the signal with a quiet verbal command. Continue to pop a treat in Champ's mouth when he does come. Gradually eliminate the verbal command but continue to praise and reward Champ for coming to you.

Using the Hand Signals

When Champ has a good understanding of the hand signals, you can start putting them together and using them in groups as part of your training sessions. Have Champ come, sit, lay down and then come again. Praise him enthusiastically and reward him with a treat. Or rearrange the order; have him lay down, then come back up to a sit, then come and lay down again. Challenge your training skills and Champ's learning and attention skills.

Off-Leash Control

One of the biggest mistakes people make with their dogs is to take them off the leash too soon. When Champ is off leash, you have very little (or no) control and Champ will learn very quickly that he can get away from you and there's nothing you can do about it. Before Champ is allowed total off-leash freedom (outside of your house or fenced-in yard), you need to make sure that his training is sound. That means that he understands the basic commands and responds to them reliably.

Champ must also be mentally mature enough to handle the responsibility of off-leash freedom. Mentally mature means that Champ is through the adolescent stage when he needs to challenge your authority (see chapter 3) and has accepted your leadership (see chapter 6).

Some dogs are not mentally adults until they are two or three years old, some even older. Until then they are still very puppylike and don't take anything seriously. There's nothing wrong with this; many people love puppies, even big puppies! However, puppies do not have the concentration, responsibility and seriousness to be allowed off-leash freedom.

The Long Leash and the Come

The long leash that was introduced in chapter 5 in the section on teaching the come command is a good training tool for teaching off-leash control. In chapter 5, you used the long leash to teach Champ to come to you when he was a distance (but within reach of the long leash) from you. Review that training session by putting Champ on the long leash and while holding one end of it, let Champ go play. When he is distracted and not paying attention to you, call him to come and back away from him so that he gets a chance to chase you. (The chase is exciting to most dogs and this will make the come more exciting.) If he doesn't immediately start to come to you, use the long leash to give him a snap and release. If he is still ignoring you, reel him in like a fish on a fishing pole. When Champ gets to you, either under his own power or yours, you must praise him. The come must be rewarded; however, if he comes to you voluntarily, the praise should be much more enthusiastic!

When Champ is responding well to the come command, let him drag the long leash behind him as he plays. Don't let him get too far away and call him back to you often. If he responds right away, praise him, offer him a treat, then release him and let him go play again. If he doesn't respond immediately, step on the long leash, grab it and repeat the teaching process.

Don't allow Champ to run and play away from your fenced yard until he is responding to the come command on the long leash every single time you call him. Make sure he will come to you when other dogs are around, when kids are playing and screaming, when teenagers are inline skating and when birds are flapping overhead. Don't make excuses for him; if he doesn't come to you on the first command, he didn't come. Plain and simple. Excuses won't matter if he ignores you, chases a cat and gets hit by a car!

Off-Leash Heel

In most public places dogs are required to be on leash; however, the off-leash heel is a required part of obedience competition. It has some practical uses, too. If Champ is well trained, you can tell him to heel and walk him to your car or the mailbox without worrying about a leash. What happens if you are out on a walk and Champ's leash breaks? Or his collar? It's happened before and will happen again. If Champ can heel by your side without a leash and collar, you won't need to panic.

Hook two leashes up to Champ's collar—his normal leash and a second, very lightweight leash. Do a watch me with treats, then practice his heel work, having him walk nicely with you as you walk slow, fast, normal and turn corners. Stop and have him sit while you praise him. Then reach down and unhook his regular leash and toss it to the ground in front of him. If Champ bounces up, thinking he's free, correct him, "Acck! I didn't release you!" and bring him back to the sit position. Hook his regular leash back up and repeat the exercise.

When Champ sits still for the leash to be tossed to the ground, continue by telling him to heel and then practice his heel work as you did with both leashes. Stop, have him sit, put the regular leash back on and repeat the whole thing again. Go back and forth between one leash and two so much that Champ won't remember what he has on. Repeat this over several training sessions. Remember to use the watch me command with treats to help keep his attention on you.

When Champ is to the point of behaving himself regardless of the leash or leashes, take off the second leash. Fold up his regular leash and tuck it under his collar over his shoulder blades, so that it is on his back. Practice his heel work. If he makes a mistake or tries to take advantage, grab the leash on his back.

Expect (and demand) the same quality of work that you expect when he's working on leash. Don't make excuses for mistakes off leash.

There's More!

There is much more that you can teach Champ. Teach him words and hand signals for directions—left, right, back and forward. Teach him some tricks; dead dog is a great trick that always makes people laugh. Or, if you're interested, get involved in some of the dog sports and activities that are discussed in the next chapter. Champ is limited only by your abilities to teach him!

CHAPTER 10

Dog Sports and Activities

o you like spending time with Champ? Is training more fun than you expected? If you like training and playing with your dog, you may want to explore some dog activities and sports. Some activities are just for fun, others are recreational or competitive, and some involve service for people.

If you also like competition, you can earn titles for your dog by competing in many of these sports. For example, if you and your dog like obedience, and decide to compete, you can earn a Companion Dog title (CD), a Companion Dog Excellent title (CDX) or a Utility Dog title (UD). And that's just the beginning!

Conformation Competition

The American Kennel Club (AKC), the United Kennel Club (UKC) and States Kennel Club all award conformation champion titles to purebred dogs, as do the kennel clubs of other countries and provinces, including Mexico, Canada, Bermuda and Puerto Rico. The requirements for each vary slightly, but basically the conformation championship is earned when a purebred dog competes against other dogs of its breed and wins. When competing, the judge compares each dog to the standard for that particular breed and chooses the dog that most closely represents this written description.

This standard is what keeps a Greyhound looking like a Greyhound and not a Rottweiler. The standard states what the dog's head should look like, how it should be shaped and what the ears should look like. It states coat type, length, color and texture as well as body size and shape, leg length and so on. Many of the standards even discuss the dog's temperament, personality and intelligence.

This is a very simplistic explanation of both conformation competition and the breed standard. There is more to the competition than this; entire books have been written about conformation competition. However, to get started you can get a copy of the standard and the complete requirements for conformation competition by writing to the kennel club with which you wish to compete.

The American Kennel Club offers only one conformation title, Champion (Ch), and is located at 51 Madison Ave., New York, NY 10010. The United Kennel Club offers the title Champion and Grand Champion, and is located at 100 E. Kilgore Road, Kalamazoo, MI 49001-5593. The States Kennel Club offers a Champion title and can be reached at P.O. Box 389, Hattiesburg, MS 39403-0389.

Obedience Competition

Obedience competition grew out of one woman's desire to demonstrate her dogs' skills and trainability. From Helen Whitehouse Walker's first obedience demonstrations in the 1920s, the sport of obedience has become one in which thousands of dogs and their owners compete each year.

To compete in obedience and earn one of the various obedience titles, a dog and his owner must work as a team to satisfactorily complete a set of exercises. Those exercises can range from the simple to the very difficult, depending on the class entered, and could include heeling on leash, heeling off leash, retrieving a thrown dumbbell, jumping a high jump, hand-signal exercises and sit and down stay with the owner out of sight.

A number of different obedience titles are available from both the American Kennel Club, the United Kennel Club and the Australian Shepherd Club of America. The AKC obedience competition is open only to purebred dogs registered with the AKC. The UKC obedience program is available to purebred and mixed-breed dogs registered with the UKC. The Australian Shepherd Club of America (ASCA) offers obedience titles from Companion Dog through Obedience Trial Champion and is available to all breeds of dogs preregistered with ASCA.

Again, this is a very simple description of competition. Write to the AKC, ASCA or UKC and ask for a copy of their obedience regulations for complete class and exercise descriptions and competition guidelines.

Canine Good Citizen

The Canine Good Citizen program was introduced by the American Kennel Club in an effort to promote and reward responsible pet ownership. The dog and owner must complete a series of ten exercises, including sitting still for petting and grooming, demonstrating an understanding of walk on a leash, sit, down and stay and an acceptance of strange dogs and people. On completion of all ten exercises, the dog is awarded the CGC title.

The CGC is open to all dogs, purebred and mixed breeds, registered or not. For more information, write to the American Kennel Club or ask your local dog obedience instructor.

Agility Titles

Agility is a fast-growing and popular dog sport. In agility, the dog must traverse a series of obstacles that might include jumps and hurdles, a teeter-totter, a sway bridge, an A-frame, a dog walk (much like an elevated balance beam) and tunnels. The dog is judged by both the manner of completing the course (safety is stressed) and how quickly this was accomplished. A variety of different classes are available, including jumping classes for different sizes of dogs, set routines with the obstacles in a certain order and classes in which the owner can decide what order to take the obstacles.

Agility titles are offered by several different organizations, including the AKC, the UKC, the United States Dog Agility Association (USDAA) and the Australian Shepherd Club of America. For more information, including class and obstacle descriptions and the location of an agility club near you, write to each of the sponsoring organizations or contact your local dog obedience instructor.

Flyball Titles

Flyball is a sport made to order for those dogs who believe tennis balls were invented for dogs, not for the sport of tennis.

In flyball, the dogs compete on a team against another team in relay style races. The dog leaves its owner, jumps a series of four hurdles, and steps on a lever that triggers a mechanism which tosses a tennis ball. The dog then

catches the ball, turns around and races back to its owner, again jumping all four hurdles. The team that finishes first, wins. Flyball has become so popular in some parts of the country that tournaments are held on a regular basis with numerous teams playing.

The North American Flyball Association (NAFA) awards three titles: Flyball Dog (FD), Flyball Dog Excellent (FDX) and Flyball Dog Champion (FDCh). For more information, write to NAFA for training and competition guidelines, as well as the location of a club near you.

Herding Titles

The ability to herd livestock is one of the most ancient and revered of canine skills. Today, herding dogs are still used on farms and ranches all over the world; however, herding has also become a recreational pastime. The American Kennel Club and the Australian Shepherd Club of America both offer herding programs, as does the United States Border Collie Handlers Association and a number of other local and regional groups.

Hunting, Retrieving and Field Events

Using dogs to assist in the hunt is mankind's oldest use of domesticated dogs and most likely contributed to the survival of both mankind and these early dogs. Today many dogs are still used to help their owners hunt for food for the table; however, for the most part, hunting has become a recreational and competitive sport.

In fact, it is a sign of the times that in many of the hunting or field sports the prey is not injured or killed. For example, in terrier trials, the rat the dogs must find is in a secure cage at the end of the tunnel, safe from escape and safe from the dogs.

There are a variety of different kinds of hunts, hunt tests and trials, ranging from coonhounds finding and treeing raccoons, packs of Beagles chasing rabbits, Labrador Retrievers bringing back ducks, spaniels flushing the birds and the pointers pointing.

Although many people don't associate them with hunting dogs, the sighthounds are some of the oldest hunting breeds known and have their own hunting competitions and titles. The competition is called lure coursing because a lure—a plastic bag—is used to entice the dogs instead of an animal. The AKC and the American Sighthound Field Association sponsor competitions.

When you write to the American Kennel Club or the United Kennel Club, specify what breed you have and what field events you are interested in. For example, if you have an English Springer Spaniel, ask for the Registration and Field Trial Rules for spaniels and the Regulations for AKC Hunting Tests for spaniels. The same guidelines are available for pointers, retrievers, Dachshunds, Beagles, coonhounds and sighthounds.

Schutzhund

Schutzhund began in the early 1900s as a test for working police dogs. Although it remains a good test for law enforcement and military working dogs, today schutzhund has become a popular recreational sport.

Dogs competing in schutzhund are scored in three areas, including protection work, obedience and tracking. The first level of competition is called

Schutzhund I and dogs passing are awarded the title SchI. Following is Schutzhund II (SchII) and Schutzhund III (SchIII). In addition, dogs can compete to earn titles in advanced tracking, temperament tests, police training, agility and endurance.

German Shepherd Dogs predominate in the sport of schutzhund; in fact, some clubs are open only to German Shepherds. Other clubs invite all working breeds of the appropriate temperament. For more information, write to the United Schutzhund Clubs of America or Landesverband DVG America.

Temperament Test

The American Temperament Test Society was founded as a means to provide breeders and trainers with a way to uniformly evaluate a dog's temperament. By using a standardized test, with each dog being tested in exactly the same manner, the test could be used as a means of comparing and evaluating potential breeding stock or future working dogs, or simply as a way for dog owners to see how their dog might react in any given situation.

The test has several parts that evaluate certain areas of the dog's temperament, including visual stimuli, auditory stimuli, the dog's attitude toward both friendly and weird strangers and the dog's sense of self-protection. Dogs that pass all areas of the test are awarded the title TT.

For more information about the test and a schedule of tests in your area, write to the American Temperament Test Society.

Therapy Dogs

Although dog owners have always known how important our dogs' companionship is to us, researchers have now discovered that our dogs are good for us, both physically and emotionally. Walking a dog gives us exercise, playing with a dog allows us to laugh and petting a dog lowers our blood pressure. Therapy dogs use this incredible bond to help nursing home residents, hospitalized patients and children in day-care centers, to name just a few.

Potential therapy dogs must like people and cannot be out of control or aggressive. Basic obedience is a must, as is socialization to wheelchairs, walkers, canes and any other equipment the dog might come into contact with during its work. There are several therapy dog organizations, each with its own testing requirements. For more information about therapy dogs, write to one or more of the organizations listed at the end of this chapter.

Tracking

Tracking dogs have been used by police departments and search-and-rescue groups for many years. A dog's nose is incredibly sensitive to scents we can't even imagine; even with today's sophisticated law enforcement equipment, sometimes the best tool is a dog's nose. Tracking is also a recreational sport. As I mentioned previously, tracking is one of the three basic parts of the sport of schutzhund. The American Kennel Club also awards two tracking titles, Tracking Dog (TD) and Tracking Dog Excellent (TDX).

Upon your request, the AKC will send you a copy of their tracking regulations. This booklet will explain the tracking tests, the titles available and how the courses are laid out.

And There's Still More!

Many of the individual breed clubs offer titles, usually in an activity that the breed has historically participated in. For example, the Saint Bernard Club of America offers titles for weight pulling—Weight Puller (WP) and Weight Puller Excellent (WPX)—and for carting: Draft Dog (DD) and Team Draft Dog (TDD).

The Alaskan Malamute Working Dog Certification Committee has established an opportunity for Malamutes and their owners to earn several different titles. Working Pack Dog (WPD) and Working Pack Dog Excellent (WPDX) require miles of backcountry hiking and packing. Titles are also available for weight-pulling Malamutes.

The Newfoundland Club of America offers titles for water-rescue work and for carting, two of the breed's historical uses. For water-rescue work, the dogs can earn the title Water Dog (WD) and Water Rescue Dog (WRD). For carting, the dogs can earn the title Draft Dog (DD) and two Newfies working together can earn Team Draft Dog (TDD).

The Dalmatian Club of America offers road trial titles, again a reflection of the breed's historical function. Dalmatians can earn the title Road Dog (RD) and Road Dog Excellent (RDX) by running with a rider on horseback or with a wagon pulled by a team of horses.

Many of the titles offered by breed clubs are usually available only to members of those specific breeds; however, many clubs have similar programs. If your breed is not listed, write to your national club and find out if they have a working program. If they don't, offer to help get one started!

Resources

Alaskan Malamute Working Dog Program, Rt. 2, Box 422, Twist, WA 98856 (weight pulling, hiking and packing, sledding: Malamutes only).

American Border Collie Association, 82 Rogers Rd., Perkinston, MS 39573 (herding: Border Collies).

American Kennel Club, 51 Madison Ave., New York, NY 10010 (conformation, obedience, Canine Good Citizen, agility, hunting, retrieving, field and den trials, lure coursing, tracking).

American Temperament Test Society, P.O. Box 397, Fenton, MO 63026 (temperament tests).

Australian Shepherd Club of America, 6091 E. State Highway 21, Bryan, TX 77808-9652 (conformation for Australian Shepherds only, obedience, agility for all breeds, herding).

Dachshund Versatility Program, Dachshund Club of America, P.O. Box 670, Cabazon, CA 92230 (conformation, obedience, field and den trials: Dachshunds only).

Dalmatian Club of America, 4390 Chickasaw Rd., Memphis, TN 38117 (road tests: Dalmatians only).

Delta Society, P.O. Box 1080, Renton, WA 98057-1080 (therapy dogs).

Jack Russell Terrier Club of America, P.O. Box 4527, Lutherville, MD 21094-4527 (terrier trials).

Landesverband DVG America, 113 Vickie Dr., Del City, OK 73115 (schutzhund).

Love on a Leash Therapy Dog Program Inc., 3809 Plaza Dr., No. 107–309, Oceanside, CA 92056 (therapy dogs).

Newfoundland Club of America, Water Work Secretary, 7481 South 3500 East, Salt Lake City, UT 84121 (water tests: Newfoundlands only). Land Work Secretary, 2461 Overlook Dr., Walnut Creek, CA 94596-3008 (carting: Newfoundlands only).

North American Flyball Association, 1 Gooch Park Dr., Barrie, Ontario, Canada, L4M 3S6 (flyball, all breeds).

States Kennel Club, P.O. Box 389, Hattiesburg, MS 39403-0389 (conformation for all breeds).

Saint Bernard Weight Pull Secretary, 12104 214th Ave. East, Sumner, WA 98390 (weight pulls: Saint Bernards only).

United Kennel Club, 100 E. Kilgore Rd., Kalamazoo, MI 49001-5593 (conformation, obedience, agility, field trials, hunting, coonhound trials, retrievers).

United Schutzhund Clubs of America, 729 Lemay Ferry Rd., St. Louis, MO 63125 (schutzhund).

United States Dog Agility Association, P.O. Box 850955, Richardson, TX 75085-0955 (agility, all breeds).

United States Border Collie Handlers' Association, Rt. 1, Box 14A, Crawford, TX 76638 (herding: Border Collies).

CHAPTER 11

Responsible Dog Ownership

There is much more to dog ownership than simply feeding and caring for a dog. Unfortunately, many times people don't know what is involved until it is too late and they find themselves overwhelmed.

A Safe Environment

Champ needs a safe place to live. That means you need to make sure there is nothing for him to get into that could harm him. Champ doesn't know that fertilizers or snail bait could kill him; he just wants to explore his world, and if dangerous substances are there, he'll get into them. Put away all fertilizers, insecticides, pesticides, paints and cleaning compounds. Put them out of reach or behind securely latched doors.

Dog-proof your house, too, and put away breakables as well as dangerous chemicals. As was mentioned earlier, don't let Champ have free run of the house, unsupervised, until he is grown up, mentally mature and well trained.

The fence around your yard or Champ's run must be secure and escape-proof. Dogs can be very clever and figure out that one leap to the woodpile could lead to a leap to the shed and over the fence. Make sure your gate is locked or securely latched, too.

Champ also needs protection from neighborhood kids who might tease him. He needs to be protected from stray dogs, coyotes and other predators, as well as other wild animals.

Health Care

Champ cannot take care of himself; that's your job. He needs a good quality food to eat, water, daily exercise and protection from the weather if he's outside for hours each day.

Develop a good working relationship with a veterinarian and allow him or her to guide your dog's health care. Make sure Champ is on a regular vaccination schedule and mark your calendar as to when booster shots are due. Find out what else is required in your area. Does your vet recommend heartworm preventative? How about Lyme Disease vaccinations?

Groom Champ on a regular basis, brushing or combing his coat thoroughly. At the same time, check for cuts, scratches, lumps, bumps or bruises so that you can either treat them or watch for future problems. Check for fleas and ticks, and if Champ has them, ask your vet or groomer for advice on how to get rid of them. Trim Champ's nails as needed, and clean his ears. If you have any questions about how to groom Champ, make an appointment with your local groomer. He or she would be more than willing to show you how to care for Champ.

Freedom from Reproduction

Has Champ been spayed or neutered yet? The pet overpopulation problem is more than simple words on paper or a phrase that Bob Barker says at the closing of every "The Price is Right" show. The reality of the problem is that thousands of dogs and cats are euthanized all over the country, every day. Too many are being born with too few homes available.

Only the best of the best should be bred. There are many genetic diseases today that are crippling or killing dogs and many of them could be reduced or prevented with more careful breeding. If you are thinking of breeding Champ, he should be the best physical specimen of his breed, according to the breed standard. He should also have the temperament required of the breed. Some breeds are supposed to be outgoing and friendly, while others are reserved and cautious with strangers. Champ should be healthy and free of any genetic defects. To determine this, your veterinarian may need to x-ray Champ's elbows and hips to check for dysplasia. Blood tests to check for hereditary diseases may also be necessary.

Champ's parents and grandparents must also be just as healthy, and the dog (or bitch) that Champ is to be bred to should be equally as sound.

In addition, you should have new homes lined up, with a monetary deposit given, for any potential puppies born. And speaking of money, responsible breeders will tell you that breeding is a losing proposition. The pregnant bitch will need veterinary prenatal care, as well as additional food and nutritional supplements. Veterinary care may be needed during the delivery and the puppies will need to see the vet. The bitch will need extra food while lactating, and the puppies will need food when mom weans them. The puppies will also need vaccinations and deworming treatments prior to going to their new homes.

Spaying (or neutering) Champ could also potentially lengthen his life. Research has shown that spaying a bitch (female) reduces significantly the incidence of cancer as the bitch grows older. The same has been shown to happen to dogs (males).

There are other benefits to spaying and neutering. When a bitch has been spayed, she no longer goes through the heat cycle and so no longer bleeds or spots, and the neighborhood male dogs no longer come calling on her. A male dog that has been neutered has less desire to escape from the yard, roam, look for bitches or fight other male dogs. The incidences of leg lifting and marking are also reduced.

There is also the social obligation of spaying or neutering Champ. Do you really need to breed Champ? Why? Are those reasons enough to justify the numbers of dogs dying each and every day?

The Legalities of Dog Ownership

Do you know what the local, regional and state laws are pertaining to dog ownership? If you don't think there are any, you're wrong! Check at your local animal control facility or library. There are laws pertaining to all sorts of things—some trivial, some ridiculous, some serious. There is probably a leash law and a regulation that says your dog must be licensed. Some localities require that you pick up after your dog should he relieve himself in public.

As a dog owner, you need to know what those laws are so that you can protect yourself and Champ. Plus, if your locality has some laws that fit the ridiculous classification, work to get them changed or appealed!

Public Behavior

Use Champ's training to ensure that he behaves himself when you are out for a walk or playing in the park. It may not be fair, but unfortunately, every dog out in public represents all other dog owners. If your dog is barking, jumping on people or behaving like a wild animal, or if you don't pick up after your dog when he relieves himself, people will react negatively to other dog owners. Many public areas are now off-limits to all dogs because of some irresponsible dog owners. However, responsible dog owners can reverse some of that damage. Show the world what a joy a well-trained dog can be!